THE COMMON MARKET

PROGRESS AND CONTROVERSY

Edited by Lawrence B. Krause

PRENTICE-HALL, Inc., Englewood Cliffs, N.J.

Current printing (last digit):

11   10   9   8   7   6   5   4

Copyright © 1964 by PRENTICE-HALL, INC., Englewood Cliffs, N.J.
All rights reserved. No part of this book may be reproduced in any form,
by mimeograph or any other means, without permission in writing from
the publishers. *Library of Congress Catalog Card Number 64-16427.*
Printed in the United States of America—C. P 15279; C 15280.

To My Wife

PREFACE

The European Common Market has commanded the attention of scholars since the Messina Conference of 1955. Unfortunately, from the point of view of scholarship, the Common Market has changed so rapidly that there has never been a good time to write about it. Developments within Europe have a way of making current writing sound like ancient history. One particularly important event, the vetoing of British membership in the Common Market, occurred after most of the articles included in the volume were written. It was felt, however, that the contribution of these articles to knowledge has in no way been diminished and they appear to have already passed the test of history.

The articles have been reproduced with only minor editorial changes and can be read as self-contained pieces. While this does most justice to the authors, it does run the risk of allowing some duplication of ideas in the volume. It was decided that this risk was worth taking. Furthermore, the British entry question was discussed by a couple of authors. This material has also been mainly retained in its original form in part because it underlines the importance of the frustration of British entry and also because the bridge between the Continent and Britain may yet be built someday.

L.B.K.

CONTENTS

ix

INTRODUCTION

THE COMMON MARKET: PROGRESS
AND CONTROVERSY

Lawrence B. Krause

The man frequently called the father of the Common Market, Jean Monnet, has said that European unity is the most important event in the West since the war. This conclusion reflects much more than normal paternal pride over a robust offspring. It is well documented on all sides. The European Common Market, officially called the European Economic Community (EEC), has affected the economic, political, and military policies of all countries and especially the United States. It has been emulated in Latin America, Africa, and even within Europe itself. It has induced other countries to try to become part of it as either full or associate members. It does indeed represent a peaceful revolution in our times.

The revolution despite its peaceful nature has not lacked controversy. For every admirer can be found a skeptic and a critic. It is hard to imagine that so fundamental a change could be otherwise. Controversy has arisen because some have been dissatisfied with the direction of the change while others have tried to deny its existence. The twofold purpose of this volume is to shed some light on the meaning of the Common Market for both member and non-member countries and also to indicate the nature of the controversy that it has raised.

WHAT IS THE COMMON MARKET?

The European Economic Community came into existence on January 1, 1958, after the Treaty of Rome was ratified by the national parliaments of France, Italy, West Germany, Belgium, Luxembourg, and the Netherlands. In November 1962, a seventh European country, Greece, became associated with the EEC and began a transition to full membership. The Community is first of all a customs union. A customs union, when fully implemented, is an arrangement whereby the members of the group agree to treat the goods produced in other member countries as if they had been produced within their own borders. Thus tariffs or other types of discrimination based on national origin cannot be placed upon imports of merchandise coming from other member countries. Within the confines of a customs union merchandise is as free to move as it is between states of the United States. The Rome Treaty provides for a gradual reduction of the barriers to trade among the member countries of the Common Market rather than their immediate removal and, therefore, the customs union will not be completed until the transition period is ended. The members of a customs union must agree to enforce a uniform barrier to the commerce of non-member countries (sometimes called third countries). Thus, the tariff levied on an American car will be the same regardless of whether the car is imported by Germany, France, or any of the other members. For the Common Market the external barriers to third countries was determined in general by taking an average of the pre-existing national tariffs of the member states. The adjustment of the old national tariffs to the level of the new Common External Tariff (CXT) will also be gradual and generally in line with the movement toward internal free trade.

The European Economic Community, however, is something beyond a simple customs union. As explained in the article by William Diebold, the Rome Treaty provides for a still closer integration of the respective economies with a full economic union as the ultimate goal. Because an economic union is more demanding in terms of the sacrifices asked of the members and the degree of divestiture of national sovereignty involved, the member countries did not want to commit themselves to it until the customs union was tried and proven effective. In general, the Rome Treaty only provided solutions to immediate problems and left for future negotiations those decisions that could be postponed.

The framers of the Common Market did not confine their thinking to economics alone. In their efforts to "establish the foundations of an ever closer union among the European peoples," * they had some sort of political union in mind also. In fact Walter Hallstein, the President of the Commission of the EEC, has been quoted on a number of occasions as saying that the Common Market is not in business but in politics. In his article, Professor Hallstein indicates the vision of political and economic progress which is the essence of the Common Market for the new Europeans. The excitement and promise of European integration accounts for the fascination with the Common Market for all observers, regardless of their previous points of view.

ORIGIN OF THE COMMON MARKET

In the article by Jean Monnet are indicated the salient features of our modern world that led to the creation of the Common Market. It is to the particular conditions of postwar Europe, however, that one must turn in order to understand how the old idea of economic integration finally became a reality. There are four motives that can be identified as being of major importance in the formation of the Common Market. First and foremost, the six original member countries of Continental Europe had all been defeated and occupied in World War II and were intent on preventing a reoccurrence of this calamity. The remarkable economic revival of West Germany gave a degree of urgency to this concern. The statesmen of Europe wanted to find a way to remove Germany as a political and military threat to her neighbors. While the Franco-German "rapprochement" seemed secure under the leadership of Adenauer in Germany, it was recognized that "der Alte" must someday accept the mortality of man. Even a formal treaty of friendship such as the one concluded between France and West Germany in 1963 provides no guarantee of peace as long as the parties are free to disregard or indeed to repudiate its provisions. The suggestion that seemed to give the

* Preamble to the *Treaty Establishing the European Economic Community.*

greatest hope of success was to form a new institution which would cement the economies of the member countries into an interdependent maze, out of which independent aggressive action by a single country would be impossible. A customs union seemed to provide such an institution.

The second motive behind the Common Market is related to the division of postwar Germany into an Eastern and a Western sector. While refusing to recognize the permanence of the separation, a realistic appraisal of the cold-war situation indicated that the chances for the reunification of Germany through peaceful methods within the foreseeable future seemed remote. With the chances of success so far-off, the understandable desire by Germans for reunification could only serve to increase East-West tensions and possibly lead to thermonuclear war. It was, therefore, desirable to find a channel for German nationalism that did not increase the war danger. Such an outlet is provided by European integration. It substitutes European nationalism for German nationalism, a goal quickly endorsed, especially by the younger generation. This is not to suggest that European integration has taken all the heat out of the reunification issue for West Germans. Quite the contrary, as long as seventeen million Germans live in the East under tyranny, the issue will not die. However, it does permit a wider range of possible solutions than would have been acceptable without it.

A third motive for establishing the Common Market was a desire to restore Europe to a place of dignity in the council of nations. In the face of such colossal powers as the United States and the Soviet Union, it was felt that individual European states had been eclipsed to the point of insignificance in the arena of international politics. If European nations needed a demonstration of how limited their freedom of action had become, the Suez crisis amply provided it. It was felt that if Europe was to become something more than a footnote to history, the individual nations would have to combine their power and speak with a unified voice. To be on a par with, and if need be, independent of both the United States and the U.S.S.R. was uppermost in the minds of at least some of the supporters of European integration. While the "third force" idea has been taken to an extreme by President De Gaulle of France, it has always been present in other forms elsewhere.

The fourth and purely economic motive for the Common Market was that it gave promise of an enhanced standard of living for the member countries. The European idea was sold to many groups mainly on the expectations of a higher rate of economic growth. Yet the economic benefits of integration have been obvious for many years and were not strong enough to overcome the obstacles to its accomplishment. It was only when the political desire for union became paramount that economic integration became possible. We shall subsequently return to the economic issues and examine them in greater detail.

If indeed the political motives did dominate the economic ones in the formation of the Common Market, one may well ask why there is so little political content in the Rome Treaty. The answer is to be found in the history of the European unity movement just prior to the deliberations leading to the Rome Treaty. As described by William Diebold, the most ambitious and direct attempt to further political unity in Europe, the proposed European Defense Community, was defeated in the French Parliament. The proponents of European unity learned from this setback that a frontal attack on national sovereignty was likely to fail. They had also previously witnessed the successful formation of a limited scheme of economic integration in the form of the European Coal and Steel Community. It was therefore decided that the way to encourage political unity was to progress toward economic integration. True economic integration would force upon the member countries such a high degree of coordination and harmonization of their national policies that political unification would necessarily develop as a natural consequence. While the Rome Treaty is limited to the creation of an economic institution, the authors believed that something more was involved—the birth of the spirit of national sacrifice for Community welfare—and that this spirit would carry the movement on to political unity.

THE UNITED STATES AND THE IDEA
OF EUROPEAN UNITY

The goal of European unity found some of its staunchest supporters in the United States. While encouragement by individuals was of long standing, the first official act by the United States to further the goal was to insist that as a condition of Marshall Plan Aid the several European countries would have to cooperate among themselves in order to make best use of their own resources. American support has continued through the birth and the subsequent years of operation of the European Economic Community. To some it seems quite natural for the United States to support the idea of European unity since in a way it tries to emulate the United States. However, it should be remembered that if there is an advantage in being a member of an exclusive economic club, then there is also a disadvantage in not being a member. The United States has supported the Common Market despite the fact that part of any success that it might achieve would be at the expense of the United States.

The basis of United States support for the Common Market rests on a number of pillars. First, the experience of the United States as a member of various military alliances has taught us the lesson that only a strong ally is a good ally and it was believed that economic integration would strengthen the member countries. With stronger allies in Europe, the over-all military position of the West vis-à-vis the Communists could be improved and Europe could also shoulder a larger share of the common defense burden and thereby give some relief to the United States. In a somewhat related but different vein, the United States was experiencing a feeling of frustration in leading a coalition of unequals in which the smaller members seemed to be irresponsible. As leader, the United States was forced to accept those burdens that other countries were unwilling or unable to accept. It was felt that with the added strength and unity of economic integration would also come to Europe a greater sense of responsibility.

There are other goals of the Free World which could be advanced by added strength and unity in Europe. Europe could increase its aid to the underdeveloped countries, take a more active role in solving international currency and commodity problems, and further the movement toward the liberalization of international trade and capital flows. Efforts devoted to all of these goals could be increased appreciably if both the economic ability and the political will are developed as a result of economic integration. Official opinion in the United States believed this to be the case and that a working partnership could result between the United States and a unified Europe.

Yet there are Americans who are critical of the Common Market. They argue that an increase in European power does not necessarily mean an increase in responsibility. The additional strength that economic integration may bring could be used to further the narrowly conceived self-interest of the member countries. It is suggested that the commercial policy of the Community might well be inward looking and protective rather than outward looking and liberal. Indeed in the early stages of integration, an inward looking policy seems more likely. The organization will have to make many difficult decisions without the benefit of a viable political structure and thus the interest of outsiders may be sacrificed in order to reach agreement among the members.

Even if political unity is achieved, the critics argue that the "New Europe" might be more competitive than cooperative with the United States. The European idea only appealed to some people because it promised more independence from America. They argue that the Common Market will certainly limit the freedom of action of the United States in both political and economic matters and they are therefore concerned at the prospect.

Finally, it is argued that even if a true partnership is achieved with good will and responsibility present on both sides, the result may not be desirable at least in the military field. The needs of defense may require immediate decisions without allowing time for consultations. How is decisive action to be taken by an organization with two heads? Contingencies will always arise for which responses will not have been prepared. Either there must be a chain of command with undivided leadership to deal with such contingencies or the military posture of the West will be weakened. While the latter possibility must obviously be avoided, the former alternative implies that in the end the partners are not truly equal, thus the dilemma of partnership.

THE ECONOMICS OF INTEGRATION: INTERNAL CONSEQUENCES

Both the advocates and the critics of the Common Market base their arguments on the belief that integration will have a marked effect upon the economies of the member countries. These beliefs have to be examined because there are skeptics who dispute this claim. Economic integration will supposedly have some immediate (static) effects upon the member countries and will also cause some changes over a longer period of time (dynamic effects).

The immediate consequences that are expected as a result of forming a customs union come directly from the internal reduction of trade barriers. With the removal of internal tariffs, inefficient producers within the Community will no longer be protected from imports coming from other member countries and therefore will have to reduce their output. Efficient producers, on the other hand, will find many new markets opening to them as the trade barriers crumble and they will be able to expand production. The expansion of efficient production and the contraction of inefficient production within each country should make everyone better off than before. Also, the prices of those products that were previously protected by high tariffs will be reduced to the benefit of all consumers. Since the Common Market also provides for the free movement of workers (and capital) between the member countries, a further gain will come from the matching of unemployed workers with available jobs.

The longer run dynamic consequences of a customs union arise from a number of considerations. With a much larger market secure against impediments to trade, a manufacturer can safely build a much larger plant than would have been possible before integration. With larger output usually comes economies of scale. Large scale machinery involving the latest technological advances can be used, even though very expensive, because the cost can be spread out over so many units. In fact with the expansion of output, cost savings of many kinds are possible which will lower the over-all cost of a unit of production. This suggests that a customs union will allow a country to use its resources more efficiently over time, increasing productivity and thereby achieving a higher rate of economic growth.

Further benefits to the economy (sometimes called external economies) are expected to flow from the movement toward large scale enterprises. Economies characterized by small firms seldom if ever have extensive financial institutions. Without these institutions, firms can only expand by reinvesting their own earnings or borrowing from those banks that might be available. This may put a severe limitation upon the growth of the entire economy if the savings of individuals do not have a channel through which they can reach business firms. If firms are induced to become larger because of economic integration, specialized financial institutions will develop concurrently because both the need and profits from providing this kind of service will increase. Similarly other kinds of specialized services such as advertising, repairing, and management counseling will be stimulated to the benefit of the economy.

The customs union will probably also increase the flow of foreign investment into the area. Foreign firms will be attracted by the larger markets and the desire to get behind the tariff wall. This may well increase the total level of investment and the rate of economic growth of the Community. Finally, the Common Market may increase the degree and intensity of competition within the Community. The increase in the number of competitors within the market combined with legislative restraints against monopolistic practices (Articles 85 and 86 of the Rome Treaty), may undermine the cartelization of European industry. If restrictive business practices are given up, then economic growth would be stimulated.

Becoming a member of a customs union, however, will put certain constraints on participating countries on how they use economic policies to achieve desired goals. The degree to which this may occur is examined by A. C. L. Day in his article on economic planning. Numerous answers are possible depending on how much economic planning is desired, the methods chosen to achieve those ends, and the degree of coordination that can be obtained among all the members.

For the arguments of the skeptics, we turn to the article by Sidney Dell. Using both theoretical and statistical analysis, he tries to undermine the kind of analysis presented above. He is joined in his skepticism by other prominent economists. In this as in other economic arguments, there is no right and wrong. Only the experience of the Common Market itself can settle this difference of opinion and even that is not certain.

THE ECONOMICS OF INTEGRATION: EXTERNAL CONSEQUENCES

Paralleling the consequences for member countries, the formation of a customs union will also have immediate and longer-run effects on non-member countries. The removal of tariffs on internal trade combined with the retention of barriers against third countries, will be to the immediate disadvantage of non-members. Each member country previously treated the commerce of all foreign countries equally, but now they levy tariffs only on the imports from non-members. Non-members may lose export sales as a result. The United States, for instance, before the Common Market started, may have been able to export cars to the Netherlands despite the Dutch tariff and German competition because both German and U.S. cars paid the same tariff when entering the Dutch market. With the advent of the EEC, the U.S. may lose sales in the Dutch market because German cars now benefit from tariff discrimination which gives them a competitive edge they did not previously have. This situation is called trade diversion and is likely to occur when the most efficient producer of a product is found outside the Common Market.

Trade diversion may either be mitigated or enhanced by the longer-run effects of the Common Market. If the dynamic consequences of economic integration do occur within the member countries, then their rate of economic growth will be raised. With greater incomes, the member countries will buy more goods from outside the Community. Also, the stimulus to growth may increase inflationary pressure within the Common Market and reduce its competitiveness in world markets. However, part of the increase in investment within the member countries will be devoted to expanding production of products previously imported from the outside. Indeed the investments made by foreign firms may well be for the purpose of producing within the Common Market the same products that these firms had been exporting to them. Whether non-member countries are hurt or helped by the Common Market will depend on the relative strengths of these opposing economic forces and on the economic policies adopted by the Common Market.

WHAT HAS THE COMMON MARKET ACCOMPLISHED?

Economic goals

We now turn from speculation over what might result from the Common Market to an analysis of what has happened in the member countries. The appraisal of the situation depends in part on whether the economic side or the political side of the Common Market is being studied and on whether one is looking from the inside out or the outside in.

As Diebold indicates, there was a great deal of concern in 1957 as to whether France with her seemingly weak economy could meet the obligations of the Common Market and in particular whether she could begin the reduction of internal tariffs scheduled to start on January 1, 1959. This concern was unwarranted. Not only has the schedule of internal tariff reductions on industrial products been met, it has been accelerated. As of July 1963, the internal tariffs had been reduced by 60% of their former level, two and a half years ahead of schedule. In January 1962, the Community agreed to the first step toward integrating the agricultural sectors of the member countries. While progress on the agricultural front has been very limited, some observers argue that any progress is remarkable in view of the difficult political situation involved. The Common Agricultural Policy and its consequences for the United States figure in the testimony of Charles S. Murphy. With the agricultural agreement, the Common Market was allowed to proceed into its second transitional stage, also on schedule. This event was certainly a milestone in the life of the Community.

These developments might be called legislative successes; their real impact depends upon their economic consequences. The Common Market has brought together a market of over 170 million people with average incomes among the highest in the world. This vast market captured the imagination of the average citizens and seems to have invigorated the businessmen within the Community. It is, therefore, no surprise to find that imports and exports among the member countries themselves increased by 98 per cent between 1958 and 1962, while their trade with the rest of the world increased by only 35 per cent in those years. Changes in the international reserve position (gold and foreign exchange holdings) of the member countries jointly provide another measure of their over-all strength in international markets. The international reserves of the member countries have increased continually during the life of the Common Market, doubling in the process and reaching a level by mid 1963 10 billion dollars higher than before the Community started.

The economic progress of the Community can also be seen in the record level of production being achieved. Between 1958 and 1962, industrial production within the member countries increased by 34 per cent or an average annual growth rate of 7.6 per cent. This compares very favorably with the 4.0 per cent growth rate found in the European countries making up the European Free Trade Association.* Even the United States starting from an artificially low level in 1958 because of the recession in that year, only had a growth of industrial production of 6.0 per cent per year to 1962, less than that of the Community. Some observers believe that this growth of industrial production and national income inside the EEC has been one of the main reasons why many non-member countries are anxious to become part of the Community.

These successes have been freely attributed by many to the operations of the Common Market. There are some, however, who are skeptical. In his article, Alexander Lamfalussy questions whether the cause of Europe's progress is really the Common Market. By comparing the experience of the individual countries before and after the formation of the Common Market, he casts some doubt on the conclusions previously drawn. This then is another unsettled issue of the Community.

Political goals

In any event, the views of the Common Market described above all come solely from looking at the economics of the Community. What progress has been made toward achieving the political goals of the Common Market? As to this question there is little room for dispute, as practically all observers recognize that there has been precious little if any progress toward political unity in the Common

---

* The seven EFTA countries are Austria, Denmark, Norway, Portugal, Sweden, Switzerland, and the United Kingdom.

Market. In many ways, this comes as a surprise. The ease with which the Rome Treaty was approved by the parliaments of the member countries including France gave promise of future political successes. All political parties supported the Treaty with the sole exception of the communists. The early economic progress of the Community seemed to set the stage for a concerted attack upon the still unsettled political and economic questions. However, the momentum was lost and the institutional structure of the Common Market is still limited to what was provided for in the Rome Treaty.

The existing institutional structure of the Common Market includes the Commission which acts as the executive, the Council of Ministers representing the governments of the member states, the Assembly representing the parliaments of the member states, and the Court of Justice which provides for the judicial needs of the Community. The people making up the Commission are supposed to represent the interests of the Community as a whole and not the individual member states from which they come, giving the EEC its supranational character. On the other hand, the real power within the Community lies in the hands of the Council of Ministers and these ministers do represent the national interests of the members.

In a real sense, the politics of the Common Market so far differs very little from that preceding the Rome Treaty. Decisions of the Council of Ministers are similar to treaties that sovereign countries might make. This is so because the decisions of the Council must be unanimously approved, and therefore, each country has a veto just as a country would have in making a treaty. While the Rome Treaty does allow some issues to be decided by qualified majority voting during the transitional period and most issues thereafter, no important issue has yet been decided over the objections of a member country. There are, however, some real differences from the pre-EEC days. First, it is always the same six countries coming together to make treaties. Second, the subjects upon which agreements are to be made have generally already been scheduled. Finally, reaching agreement in the main is mandatory if progress within the Community is to be maintained.

The reason why there has not been any noticeable progress toward political unity can be traced to a difference of opinion that developed quite early in the life of the Community as to the desired form of political unity. The moving spirits of the European idea such as Jean Monnet, Paul-Henri Spaak, Walter Hallstein, and others clearly had a federal form of government in mind for the "New Europe." The member states would be obliged to give up a great deal of national sovereignty to a supranational government. While the old national states would not disappear under this plan, they would be no more powerful than the several states of the United States. It was recognized that this desired form of government could not be brought about rapidly, indeed the United States operated under the Articles of Confederation before forming a federal union; however, the logic of the movement had a strong central government as its ultimate goal. One can argue further that the idea of an Atlantic Partnership requires such a political organization in Europe.

In opposition to the federalist idea, President De Gaulle of France with some scattered support elsewhere in Europe, put forth the belief that political unity in Europe should develop without destroying the essential sovereignty of the old national states. He believes that the national states are the best unit for furthering economic and political power and wants to see them preserved close to their present form. Political unity could be enhanced while maintaining national sovereignty by institutionalizing consultations and cooperation among governments along the lines of the Franco-German Treaty of 1963. The invitation has been extended to the other Common Market countries to join this pact, but so far it has not been accepted. Max Beloff examines this problem in his article and possibly indicates a way around this dilemma. While these two ideas as to European unity may be ultimately unreconcilable, in their extreme forms, advancement toward unity could proceed without committing the Common Market to either path. In fact, up to January 1963, it appeared as if some progress had been made. The member countries seemed to share a determination to agree, and this made the Common Market work. This progress, however, has subsequently stopped because of the crisis over the relationship of Great Britain to the Common Market.

The inability to make significant progress toward political unity has many serious consequences, as the institutions set up by the Rome Treaty have many deficiencies. Of primary importance has been the fact that reaching unanimous agreement within the Council of Ministers among the six countries has been extremely difficult. The decision-making process is very cumbersome and the negotiations required to reach agreement are long and painful. As an example, one can point to the months of negotiations required to decide how much grain is needed to raise a chicken from birth to maturity for market. This seemingly technical question had to be decided at the highest political level. When unanimous consent is required, an individual country can make gains at the expense of the others by being adamant and uncompromising. Nor does there appear to be much room for bargaining between countries as each country's position is itself the result of a delicate balancing of national interests that are hard to reconcile. The Council of Ministers faces the task of settling each issue to the satisfaction of every country individually, or alternatively, widening the number of issues settled simultaneously to allow some horse trading between countries. If this latter alternative is chosen, the negotiations are really drawn out because of the complexity of the issues at hand.

The consequences of having such a difficult decision-making process are not favorable, particularly for non-member countries. First, with so many internal interests to satisfy, little attention is given to the implications of policy decisions for non-members. Since the Council of Ministers must reconcile the conflicting agricultural interests of France and Germany, they have not given proper attention to the legitimate interests of American farmers in their deliberations. Second, once a decision is made, it is very difficult to get it reversed even in the face of unexpectedly adverse consequences. Reconsidering issues amounts to opening old wounds which the Ministers are not wont to do. Third, it is clear that decisions are not made on issues until they are obviously critical for the Community as a whole or for one of the member countries. There are so many problems facing the Community that if a policy position is not needed for six months, it is considered long range policy. As a result, some important problems are not given proper attention until they reach a crisis stage when solutions are more difficult to find. In summary, one can say that the decision-making process itself has so far prevented the Community from adopting positions of concerted responsibility.

EXTERNAL CONSEQUENCES OF THE COMMON MARKET

Other Europe

Up to now we have examined the Common Market primarily from the point of view of its members. Now we turn to look at the Common Market through the eyes of countries that are not members. The neighboring states of the Common Market within Europe were the ones most immediately concerned and affected by the formation of the EEC. These countries quite naturally carry on a great deal of trade with the members and have other close commercial ties with them. Some of them, like Great Britain, did not choose to be part of the integration movement, while others found their political position of neutrality prevented them from participating. In any event, they all became greatly concerned over their economic prospects when it became clear that the Rome Treaty was going to be ratified.

As explained by Diebold, the other European countries under the leadership of Great Britain first tried to prevent the splitting of Europe by proposing an all embracing free trade area, but when that attempt failed, they formed a rival organization called the European Free Trade Association (EFTA).* This organization, however, cannot compensate the members for being excluded from the EEC. As is seen in Table 1, most of the EFTA countries have greater trade flows with the EEC than they do with other EFTA countries. For Austria and Switzerland, this difference is most marked.

The realization that more could be gained by becoming a member of the Common Market than by staying outside finally led to a policy reversal within Great Britain and in August 1961, the Macmillan Government made formal application for membership. Along with Britain, the other members of EFTA (except Portugal and Finland) plus Ireland and Spain also sought a connection with the EEC. The negotiations that ensued were long and difficult. The prospects of British entry raised many new problems for the Community, and also emphasized the unresolved questions already exist-

---

* The original members of EFTA included Austria, Denmark, Norway, Portugal, Sweden, Switzerland, and the United Kingdom. Subsequently, Finland became an associate member.

Table 1

Percentage distribution of the international trade of the members
of the European Free Trade Association by trading partners
(exports plus imports for 1962)

Partner country	Other EFTA	EEC	Others	Total
Austria	14.4	55.8	29.8	100.0
Denmark	42.8	34.1	23.1	100.0
Finland	31.3	31.9	36.8	100.0
Norway	41.4	30.0	28.6	100.0
Portugal	22.3	31.9	45.8	100.0
Sweden	33.6	37.3	29.1	100.0
Switzerland	15.2	54.5	30.3	100.0
United Kingdom	12.8	18.1	69.1	100.0
EFTA as a whole	20.9	29.7	49.4	100.0

Source: EFTA Bulletin (Geneva), April 1963.

ing. Progress seemed to have been made in the negotiations on some,
but by no means all of the problems involved. As revealed in the
article by Paul-Henri Spaak, the end of the negotiations came suddenly on January 14, 1963 when President De Gaulle in a press
conference indicated that France was vetoing British entry at least
for the present time.

No completely satisfactory alternative has been presented to replace the idea of an expanded Common Market. The EFTA organization has been given a lease on life and has been strengthened
through moves to increase its agricultural coverage and to further
reduce industrial tariffs. Within the Common Market itself, a crisis
of confidence has resulted. It may well be that the breach within
Europe can only be healed with help of policy initiatives coming
from outside Europe, possibly from the United States.

Africa

The non-European area most intimately involved with European
integration has been Africa. Many of the new states of Africa
formerly had colonial ties with the member countries of the EEC
(mainly France) and their economies reflected this dependent sta-

tus. When the Rome Treaty was written, most of these countries had not yet reached independence and special provisions were made for them in an annex to the Treaty. In essence, the Community as a whole accepted the responsibilities toward the African areas formerly borne by the individual member countries. Benefits provided in the annex included economic aid plus a favored status for imports coming into the EEC from them. It was recognized that after independence, the African countries would want to negotiate their ties to the EEC for themselves, so the provisions of the annex were limited to five years. During 1963, a new treaty was negotiated which replaced the annex with somewhat similar provisions.

While the provisions of the annex and the subsequent treaty were of unquestioned benefit to the African countries involved, this did not prevent a great deal of controversy from arising. Within the associated countries themselves, some political leaders argued that their continued economic dependence on Europe put them in a neo-colonial position which severely limited their sovereignty. One country, Guinea, after becoming independent, refused to become associated with the EEC and left the franc area altogether. However, all of the other former French territories have remained associated.

Further controversy has been generated, however, because not all African countries have been offered association with the EEC. The former British colonies and other African countries are not included. As explained in the article by Ali Mazrui, this has caused many economic and political problems for these new nations. On the economic side, the trade preferences granted the associated African countries have weakened the competitive position of the non-associated countries in the EEC market. Ghana, for instance, must now sell her cocoa in West Germany burdened by a tariff which is not levied on cocoa coming from Cameroon. While no one is critical of an advanced country helping a less developed country, resentment is caused when the prosperity of one less developed country is furthered at the expense of another.

The political problems involved are no less acute. Recognizing that modern nations require a larger population and economic base than is now found in most African countries, there has been general support for the movement to overcome the Balkanization of Africa in one way or another. However, the split between the associated and the non-associated reinforcing the natural cleavage between French and English speaking countries has effectively thwarted all pan-African movements.

Latin America and Asia

It is probably a fair generalization to say that the birth of the European Economic Community was greeted with misgivings and concern in Latin America and Asia. The apprehension stemmed primarily from economic considerations, but also had a political root. On the economic side, the Latin American countries faced the same sort of discrimination in selling tropical agricultural commodities in the Community as the non-associated African countries. Producers of coffee, cocoa, and bananas became alarmed at the prospect of the former French colonial areas taking over their markets in the Common Market because of tariff discriminations. If the privileged position in the European market led to an unwarranted expansion of production of tropical products in Africa as seemed likely, then the Latin Americans would suffer further as a result of a decline in world market prices of their products. While the dire predictions of earlier years are yet to be realized, there are still grounds for concern. Some of the immediate impact of the discriminatory tariffs have been mitigated because the EEC has granted tariff free or tariff reduced quotas to the member countries to continue importing these products from traditional suppliers. However, the quotas are only temporary. Furthermore the long gestation period required to bring new tropical agricultural products into production may mean that the major increase in African output is yet to come.

The immediate response of Latin America to the challenge of the Common Market was to start an integration movement of its own. The Latin American Free Trade Association (LAFTA) was formed in the belief that a united Latin America would be in a stronger bargaining position in world markets and also it was hoped that the success that economic integration had brought to Europe could be transported to the Americas. To date LAFTA has provided more promise than reality. A great many difficult problems remain to be solved before the organization can have any marked effect.

The reaction of Asia to the Common Market, except for Japan, was rather subdued until Great Britain decided to join, and then the fears heard elsewhere were sounded with a loud voice. Even after the rejection of the British application, these fears have not been completely calmed. In part they reflect a belief that Britain may subsequently gain entry into the EEC and in part reflect dissatisfaction with the efforts Europe is making to help the less developed countries expand their commercial exports. There is no doubt that Europe could do more on this score, but the question of whether Europe should reduce her protection of inefficient domestic industries to the benefit of Asia is another controversial issue surrounding the Community.

The position of Japan is a good bit different. Japanese exports have been effectively discriminated against by all European countries including Great Britain since the war. The Common Market, therefore, could not retard exports that did not exist. On the other hand, the Rome Treaty does imply that these discriminations will now be harder to remove than they might have been otherwise. This presumption arises from the fact that the member countries are not free to make separate commercial policy decisions. All trade measures must be approved by the Community as a whole and this is likely to slow down the pace of liberalization toward Japan rather considerably. This is not to suggest that no progress can be made, but it will simply be more difficult.

The political misgivings of the Japanese toward the Common Market stem from the same source as those of the Latin Americans. Both are concerned by the prospect that European developments will so absorb the attention of the United States that the U.S. will overlook its friends and responsibilities elsewhere. Atlantic partnership or an Atlantic Community would exclude both the Japanese and the Latin Americans. While the partnership might well hold out a great deal of promise for helping other countries, it is only natural for these other countries to be distrustful of a decision-making apparatus in which they have no voice.

The United States

By endorsing the idea of European integration so completely and by giving it so much encouragement, the United States lost most of its bargaining power to mold the European Economic Community in a form it desired. It is not clear, however, whether the United States would have wanted to change the Rome Treaty even if it could. The United States could not consider joining the Common Market, nor even seek a special deal with it. We could at best only hope for a satisfactory working arrangement and for this the Rome Treaty seemed quite adequate. It is not the policies and procedures that were agreed to at the start which will determine whether the Common Market will yield a gain or a loss for the United States, but the policies that are to follow.

The article by Irving Kravis identifies the economic and political interests of the United States that are affected by the Common Market. Needless to say, these effects have been substantial in the past and will become even larger in the future.

The Common Market has presented the United States with a series of economic and political challenges. On the economic side, the first challenge was felt by our exporters in their efforts to sell in the Community. The tariff discriminations growing out of the Common Market were bound to affect the United States because we are the largest single exporting nation in the world. The loss of competitiveness implied thereby further weakened our balance of payments position which was already far from satisfactory. Our manufactured products which compete with Germany and France for the European market will be put under increasing pressure as internal tariffs are removed and the external tariff wall is erected. However, it is with respect to American agricultural exports that the Common Market will be most damaging. As explained in the testimony of Charles S. Murphy, the common agricultural policy (CAP) poses a very great threat to many of our temperate zone agricultural products. In fact, we have already witnessed a precipitous decline in our poultry exports as a direct result of the CAP. Furthermore, the preferences granted the associated African countries compromises some of our tropical agricultural exports.

A second challenge to American exports comes about indirectly via third countries. If the Common Market is successful in redirecting its purchases away from Latin America to Africa, then the United States will be greatly affected. Latin American countries are very good customers of the United States. If their exports earnings are reduced, then they will purchase less imports in general and from the United States in particular. The corresponding increase in exports of the African areas will not lead to a compensating expansion of American sales there because the Africans buy an overwhelming percentage of their imports from Europe. Thus, the United States will either lose exports sales to Latin America, or we will be forced to increase our economic aid to them in order to maintain the old export level.

The third economic challenge comes from the inducement that the Common Market provides for American companies to make direct investments behind the tariff wall. U.S. direct investments in Europe have risen from a level of about $200 million per year before the Common Market to an average level of about $800 million in 1960-62. While not all of this investment has gone into the EEC directly, most of the growth has been invested within the Community and even some investments in the U.K. were motivated on the assumption that the British would join. While foreign direct investment is not necessarily bad for the United States, it could reduce our domestic rate of growth if the investment made in Europe reduced domestic investment or it could cause us some short-run balance of payments difficulties.

The fourth economic challenge, and the term challenge may not be appropriate in this case, comes from the strategic power that the member countries have in dealing with international monetary matters. The member countries, particularly France, West Germany, and Italy, have been the surplus countries accumulating dollars as a result of deficits in the U.S. balance of payments. Whether the United States loses gold or not depends on decisions made by the governments of these countries. The United States must convince these governments to continue to hold dollars rather than gold if the present international monetary mechanism is to be continued. In this sense, the economic integration of these countries is a challenge to us.

Turning to the political side, the Common Market is in a position to challenge the leadership of the United States in the free world to the degree that it is able to develop political unity. As noted previously, the United States has indeed welcomed this challenge. While leadership does impose responsibilities on the United States, it also allows certain freedom of action whose passing is cause for some mourning. The implications of the Common Market for the NATO military alliance as explained in the article by Walter Hallstein give an indication of what is involved.

The United States has reacted to these challenges in a somewhat surprising manner. The United States might have followed a strategy of putting pressure on the Common Market at each and every point where our influence can be felt in an effort to mitigate the adverse economic consequences which integration has brought and done so without concern to the interests of other non-member countries. We also might have attempted to bolster the divisive elements within Europe in order to maintain our political and military leadership. While such a strategy would raise longer run risks in return for immediate gains, a policy of expediency would contain a great deal of logic in view of the difficult position of the United States. Faced with unemployment at home, the United States is inhibited from using domestic restraint in dealing with its international problem of the balance of payments and is thus forced to seek alternative remedies. Even the European countries who would have been adversely affected would have understood if the United States took a strictly national point of view in dealing with the Common Market. Similarly, the United States could have been excused for wanting to postpone facing the challenge to its political leadership in view of the rapidly changing world power situation following the schism within the communist bloc. Yet, the United States did not choose the road of expediency, but instead followed a much more enlightened path.

The United States faced the economic challenge of the Common Market by taking a world point of view. The development of regional trading blocs reversed the movement toward multilateral liberalization of international trade which had advanced since the war. The advantages of the multilateral approach means that the reversal is not desirable. The United States struck a mighty blow for multilateralism and non-discrimination by empowering the President via the Trade Expansion Act of 1962 to seek worldwide solutions to the Common Market challenge. In brief, the Trade Expansion Act allows the United States to enter into negotiations with other countries under the auspices of the General Agreement on Tariffs and

Trade (GATT) for the purpose of agreeing to a general reduction of trade barriers. The tariff reductions that might result from such negotiations would be applicable to all free world countries under the rules of GATT, the so-called "Most Favored Nations Principle." The United States, therefore, has responded to the challenge of the Common Market in a way that would benefit all non-member countries, not just the United States.

The major goal sought at the GATT negotiations is a substantial reduction of the common external tariff (CXT) of the Common Market. With a reduction of the CXT, tariff discriminations against products of all non-member countries would be lessened. This not only would allow greater U.S. exports to the EEC, it would also encourage Japanese and Latin American sales to Europe. Furthermore, the attraction of Europe as a place for American companies to make direct investment would be lessened as European protectionism is reduced. The main compensation offered the Common Market to induce them to reduce tariffs is the pledge by the United States to reduce our tariffs by an equal amount. Other advanced countries of GATT would also be expected to similarly reduce their barriers to trade which in the aggregate would amount to a substantial liberalization. If successful, the GATT negotiations would go a long way toward meeting the economic challenge of the Common Market.

The United States has had little opportunity to come to grips with the challenge of the Common Market to our political and military leadership. Because internal political unity within the EEC has not advanced, the United States has no choice but to deal with the individual governments of the member countries. The member countries must empower the Commission of the EEC (or some other unit) to negotiate for the Community as a whole if they are to speak with a single voice and this they have been unwilling to do. Yet, the strains of the Western Alliance are already present. So far the dissatisfaction with the monopoly of American leadership has appeared as refusals by individual governments (mainly France) to be bound by NATO decisions. A dissent cannot become a positive force, however, until feasible alternatives are presented and none has appeared. For example, the effort by the United States to share our military leadership through a schema of a multinational nuclear force was rejected by some countries without revoking an alternative proposal. It seems, therefore, that solutions to the political challenge must wait until the development of political unity in Europe goes forward.

PROSPECTS FOR THE FUTURE

The Common Market has given birth to many more problems than solutions. The remaining problems will have to be dealt with. A movement that depends on momentum for success such as the Common Market cannot long rest on the laurels of previous accomplishments even though they are substantial. However, as pointed out by Paul-Henri Spaak, the political climate within the Community following the veto of the British application for membership is not a good one for problem solving. The wisdom of waiting for the removal of a temporary obstacle to progress rather than changing course is compelling. On the other hand, the longer a single hurdle blocks the path of progress, the more likely it is that other hurdles will appear. No effort can be spared as long as there is some hope for reaching effective solutions to the problems at hand.

The best strategy would seem to be to press forward on those problems for which solutions seem most attainable. If a direct attack on political unity cannot succeed even though this is the most basic need of the Community, then efforts must be directed to the outstanding economic questions. The Kennedy round of trade negotiations within the GATT seems to provide such an opportuntiy.

One cannot overemphasize the importance of the trade negotiations for the Common Market for they provide both an internal and external test of the Community. The negotiations underscore some of the conflicts that divide the member countries. The agricultural question is the most important, but not the only case in point. The negotiations will test whether national interests have so frozen the policies of the member countries that there is no room left for compromise, or whether the Community spirit so in evidence before January 1963 can be revived.

On the external side, the test will be no less severe. Critics of the Common Market have long said that the Community is basically protectionist minded and they point to the common agricultural policy to illustrate their position. If this is so, then the Common Market will try to prevent the successful completion of the Kennedy round. However, many observers dispute this claim and state that the Community is on balance liberal to non-member countries. The intentions of the EEC as specified in the Rome Treaty and the public statements of the EEC Commission give some support to this belief. Furthermore, the EEC has participated actively in one successful round of tariff negotiations, the Dillon round, and has taken other small measures to lessen its adverse impact on the rest of the world. If the optimists are correct, then the EEC will seek real solutions to the problems that now seem to bar the way to a successful negotiation.

The Kennedy round of trade negotiations has political as well as economic significance. One need only glance at some of the possibilities that might follow a failure of the negotiations to recognize the political stakes involved. Without the possibility of adjustments within a framework of tariff reductions, the many difficulties over tariffs such as the U.S. concern over poultry, tobacco, and canned fruits and the European concern over chemicals and carpets could lead to a kind of trade war in which retaliatory tariff increases would become commonplace. Furthermore, if the Common Market became insensitive to its effects on non-members, it is conceivable that the non-members themselves might find ways within or outside of GATT rules to discriminate against the EEC. Clearly such aggressive commercial relations would undermine our political and military alliance.

Lest one lose a sense of perspective in judging the difficulty of current problems facing the free world, we should compare our present situation to past history. Within two decades following World War I, the international economy had been plagued by a worldwide depression, disrupted by successive waves of unilaterally imposed tariff increases and competitive currency devaluations, and by the institution of a vicious system of bilateral trading, and the political and military situation of Europe had deteriorated to the point of a new war. We have avoided these calamities following World War II. Cooperation among the free nations has replaced the "beggar my neighbor" policies of earlier years. Today's problems are difficult, but we have met equally difficult problems in the past and we need not be pessimistic over the possibility of finding mutually beneficial solutions now.

SUGGESTED READINGS

Max Beloff, *The United States and the Unity of Europe* (Washington, D.C.: The Brookings Institution, 1963)

Isaiah Frank, *The European Common Market* (New York: Frederick A. Praeger, 1961)

Walter Hallstein, *United Europe, Challenge and Opportunity* (Cambridge, Mass.: Harvard University Press, 1962)

Christian A. Herter, *Toward an Atlantic Community* (New York: Harper & Row, Publishers, 1963)

Uwe W. Kitzinger, *The Challenge of the Common Market* (Oxford: Basil Blackwell, 1961)

George Lichtheim, *The New Europe, Today and Tomorrow* (New York: Frederick A. Praeger, 1963)

Richard Mayne, *The Community of Europe* (New York: W. W. Norton & Co., Inc., 1963)

Pierre Uri, *Partnership for Progress* (New York: Harper & Row, Publishers, 1963)

PART I

History and Vision of European Integration

THE PROCESS OF EUROPEAN INTEGRATION

William Diebold, Jr.

William Diebold, Jr. is Director of Economic Studies of the Council on Foreign Relations. He has been at the Council since 1947 and has occasionally been a visiting lecturer at Columbia University. In this article, Mr. Diebold traces the history of the European integration movement step by step from the start of the Organization for European Economic Cooperation to the formation of the European Economic Community. He describes the content of the Rome Treaty and the institutions which it created. The progress achieved by the Common Market from birth to mid-1962 is set forth and the article concludes with a discussion of the relations of Britain and the United States to the Community.

The *limes* of the Roman Empire, the achievement of Charlemagne, the ideas of Sully, Kant, William Penn, and others—these are the conventional starting places for articles on European integration. Certainly the common elements in the cultural and political heritage of Europe have played their part in making the events of the last 15 years possible. But a major part of the European cultural heritage is nationalism and its corollaries, national diversity, conflict of interest, and friction. This makes all the more dramatic the way in which European countries have, since the war, increasingly joined together in common efforts, yielded national powers to international

"The Process of European Integration" by William Diebold, Jr. from *Current History* (March 1962). Reprinted by permission of Current History, Inc.

bodies and, indeed, made the reaching of agreement among themselves a major aim of policy. The governments that have done these things have not ceased to be national nor have any new international bodies replaced them as the main centers of political power in Europe. Integration has been largely a process of reinterpreting national interests.

This reinterpretation has been influenced by a number of familiar facts and views, such as the relative decline of Europe's power in the world, the ending of empires, the belief that the individual nation–states of Europe could no longer provide adequately for the security and welfare of their people, the Soviet threat, and a sense of the advantages of large, more or less unified, economic units, comparable in scale to those of the United States and the Soviet Union.

Unofficial organizations did much to foster ideas of European unification. First the European Movement and since 1955 Jean Monnet's Action Committee for a United States of Europe have been the most important of these organizations, but there is scarcely a shade of political opinion or an economic or functional interest that has not been represented in the roster of bodies favoring one or another brand of the European ideal. Just how important these groups have been is hard to say. In some of them people came together who were able to influence the policies of their own countries, as civil servants or intellectuals, in politics or economic life. Some groups produced plans and proposals that governments had to take into account. The whole movement did much to establish a climate of opinion which helped governments get support when they took steps toward integration.

It has been the national governments, however, that took the decisions and adopted the policies that make up the process of integration. Nationalism is not dead in Europe, but it has changed some of its ways.

Though ideas about uniting Europe were in the air, the immediate postwar concern of each country was its own economic and political reconstruction. Even Benelux, a customs union first agreed on in 1944, was slow to take shape because Belgium and the Netherlands faced different problems. When the first round of reconstruction loans from the United States proved inadequate, the stage was set for the Marshall Plan. To justify massive American aid, said Washington, Europe would have to make the greatest possible use of its own resources. That would require close cooperation and, in particular, a breaking of the barriers to the exchange of goods inside Europe.

In these circumstances, most of the countries of Western Europe joined in the first major step toward integration, the creation of the Organization for European Economic Cooperation (OEEC) and the exchange of extensive and fairly detailed pledges of cooperation. The OEEC lacked the authority some had tried to give it; it did not produce a unified European recovery program; its limited efforts to coordinate investment had small results. Nevertheless the OEEC brought intra-European economic cooperation to an unprecedented level and paved the way for what followed.

Two of the major accomplishments of the OEEC were the progressive removal of quotas on trade among the members and the establishment of the European Payments Union (EPU) which financed some of that trade and removed many of the restrictions of bilateralism. Less clearly visible than these measures was a third major accomplishment. In connection with the allocation of American aid, the annual review of each country's economy, and some EPU operations, national policies, and performance were exposed to close criticism from other countries and from the OEEC secretariat under Robert Marjolin. These confrontations did much to develop the practice of economic cooperation and the sense of common interests and standards. By creating the need to "think multilaterally," as one regular participant put it, this process made an important contribution to integration.

Neither the Brussels Treaty Organization formed in 1948, nor the Council of Europe, created in 1949, played a great part in economic integration. They also did not satisfy the hopes of some that they would provide the dynamics for broader political integration. By 1950 the belief was growing that no organization that depended on unanimous consent for most action, as the OEEC and the Council of Europe did, was going to move Europe much farther along the road of integration.

THE EMERGENCE OF THE SIX

What Western Europe as a whole could not do, "Little Europe" began. On May 9, 1950, Robert Schuman, the French Foreign Minister, proposed a pooling of Europe's coal and steel industries "under a common High Authority." The step was radical. It not only called for free trade in basic products but proposed putting industries that were traditionally the sinews of war largely under the control of a new "supranational" body to which governments would surrender important powers. Such ideas had been discussed before. The remarkable thing was that a major power should accept them as policy. A number of factors explained the French decision. By far the most important was the need for a new approach to an old problem —Germany.

The victors' original postwar policies toward Germany had been abandoned. Partition, Soviet pressure, the responsibilities of occupation and the effort to strengthen Western Europe all militated against plans to keep the German economy weak. It became very clear that a depressed Germany was a drag on the Western European economy. With economic revival would come not only strength but also autonomy. How could Germany's neighbors guard against the threat that sometime in the future a powerful independent Germany might again be a danger to them—with or without the eastern regions that were under Soviet control?

The Schuman Plan answered the question by offering Germany partnership. If international control over basic industries could not be imposed, perhaps it could be won by reciprocal French acceptance of terms that offered advantages to both countries. More important than any specific features of the pooling and supranational control was the prospect of starting a process through which Germany would become so intertwined with the rest of Western Europe that it would resist any future temptation to turn on its partners. The Germans responded favorably for a variety of reasons, some connected with the prospect of regaining an equal status in Europe and freeing their country from the special disabilities defeat had put on it and some arising from the same "European" sentiments that existed in other countries.

To no one's surprise, the British refused to take part in the Schuman Plan negotiations. France, Germany, Italy, and the Benelux countries agreed on a treaty embodying the main elements of Schuman's original proposal, in spite of serious opposition from economic and political groups. The European Coal and Steel Community (ECSC) came into existence in 1952 and in a short while tariffs and quotas on the movement of coal, steel, and iron ore within the Community were removed, subsidies tapered off, and a number of measures were taken to end discriminatory freight rates. Common rules were established for price policies and the new Community made progress in regulating cartels and concentrations.

A high level of demand during most of the period helped greatly. There was far less disturbance to production and employment than many expected. Measures to rationalize high-cost coal production were not very effective until after 1958 when coal surpluses put pressure on producers, especially in Belgium and Germany. At that point, although the Community continued to provide financial assistance, the main decisions were made by the governments. Not yet solved, these problems showed the limitations of partial integration and strengthened efforts to establish coordinated energy policies regulating oil as well as coal.

One of the great innovations of the Schuman Plan was the creation of supranational bodies with real but limited powers. The High Authority—which even had the ability to tax—used its powers with caution, seeking to lead more than to command. Many of its actions required the consent of the governments, in law or in fact. In the intergovernmental Council of Ministers, the nations of the Community developed new ways of working together. In the Assembly, members of the parliaments of the six countries grouped themselves according to political persuasion rather than national views.

Though its powers were only advisory, the Assembly became a center of pressure for stronger measures of integration and more often supported the High Authority than the member governments. Industry and labor were represented in a Consultative Committee while a supranational Court of Justice adjudicated cases involving the actions of governments and the High Authority. In practice the Community proved to have not a clear-cut division of powers such as the language of the treaty might suggest, but a mixed system in which national, international, supranational, and private power were intricately mixed in changing combinations.

SETBACK AND REPRISE

While the coal and steel treaty was being negotiated, American and British pressure for rearming Germany presented France with a problem it had wanted to avoid. The French reacted by proposing a twin of the Schuman Plan. The new Pleven Plan called for a European Defense Community in which national military forces would be integrated with those of other countries and subjected to something very like supranational command. Later, a looser proposal for a European Political Community was added to meet the logical need for giving unified direction to a unified command. A treaty embodying these ideas was accepted by the other five countries of Little Europe—and then turned down by France in 1954. Through British initiative the Western European Union was formed, in which Germany and Italy joined the Brussels Treaty powers. While providing a framework for dealing with security matters, WEU remained intergovernmental. It seemed as if the tide of close integration were receding.

It was something of a surprise, then, when the foreign ministers of the Six reached sufficient agreement at Messina in June, 1955, to charge a commission under Paul-Henri Spaak with the task of preparing further measures of integration. Out of this effort came the twin Treaties of Rome, signed in March, 1957, which created the European Atomic Energy Community (Euratom) and the European Economic Community (EEC).

Euratom, while it has proved to be a useful, working organization that has saved Europe time and money through cooperative research programs, has been less important than was expected because changes in the world's fuel economy postponed the time when atomic energy would be a paying proposition in Western Europe. In contrast, the EEC, the Common Market, has become firmly established sooner than could be expected and has developed such momentum that it is now a force for change not only among its six members but for Britain and a good part of the outside world as well.

In a treaty too long and intricate to be fully summarized here, the six countries agreed on many things. The most concrete were a series of steps that would create a customs union, with no barriers to trade among themselves, and a common tariff on imports from the rest of the world. Living up to the idea that they were creating an economic community and not just a new trade bloc, the six governments also agreed, but in more general terms, to provide for free movement of labor and capital, to coordinate their financial and economic policies, to establish common rules concerning competition and to take other steps that would draw their economies closer together. Two funds were established to help finance investment and economic adaptation in Europe and to aid overseas territories associated with the Community—mostly French-speaking Africa.

Like the Coal and Steel Community EEC has an intergovernmental Council of Ministers and a supranational, or independent, executive, the European Economic Commission. On paper the Commission is weaker than the High Authority, but the provisions of the Rome Treaty seem not too different from the allocation of power that has emerged in practice in the ECSC. The same Court and Assembly now serve all three Communities.

Although it is often said that the ultimate aim of the Six is to establish some kind of United States of Europe, their treaty does not say so. Its preamble speaks of a determination "to establish the foundations of an even closer union among the European peoples"— and that is about all. It is true, though, that many of the champions of European integration have had their eyes on future political integration and that the logic that has brought the Six this far points ahead. The governments have always made it clear that their main motives in joining together were broadly political.

PROGRESS IN THE COMMON MARKET

To create the customs union, the treaty allowed a period of twelve years during which tariffs were to be reduced according to a schedule; it provided several escape clauses which could extend the period to fifteen years. Familiar with the difficulties of removing long-established trade barriers and aware of the hard bargaining and extensive compromising that had gone into the drafting of the treaty, many observers thought it only realistic to suppose that the process would move as slowly as was legal and perhaps more slowly than that. Instead, the Six have moved ahead more rapidly than the original schedule called for and there is a good chance that further acceleration will be agreed on during the next two years. This development is of the utmost importance. Now one must assume that the customs union will almost certainly be created, and before too long. Moreover, the acceleration has demonstrated a degree of solidarity in the Community that has to be reckoned with as a new fact in the world. It was this as much as anything that forced the British to re-examine their policy toward Europe.

Three closely connected developments made the acceleration possible: prosperity, the reaction of business, and the changed position of France. These factors are likely to continue to have an important bearing on the progress of the Community.

The 1950's were a time of great prosperity and economic growth for Western Europe. A formal seal was put on the regained economic strength of the area when its principal currencies were made convertible for non-residents in December, 1958. Economic expansion, and the expectation that it would continue, made it easier to take the first steps to cut tariffs (and even to extend some of the benefits to outside countries) than if the threat of unemployment and unprofitability had hung over every industry.

The attitude of businessmen was also affected. Many of them had opposed the Common Market or worried about what it would do. After the Community came into being at the beginning of 1958 they rushed to meet the inevitable. In great numbers, businessmen seem to have reasoned that if tariffs were to disappear by stages, they might as well prepare immediately to meet new competition and to establish themselves in the foreign markets that would later be fully opened to them. New investments, trade and marketing drives, agreements with producers in other EEC countries all reflected this view. Since the businessmen were behaving as if the Common Market were just around the corner, not a decade and more off, there was obviously no need for the governments to go slow.

Put this way, it sounds as if prosperity created the Common Market and not the Common Market prosperity. That is largely correct. The frequently-heard converse, that Europe is prosperous because of the Common Market, is much harder to demonstrate. At least until about 1961 the amount of tariff reduction was not great enough to explain the rate of expansion. Still, business behavior in anticipation of the Common Market undoubtedly contributed to the boom, especially by stimulating investment. Economically, we can argue long about cause and effect. Historically, the important thing is that prosperity and the Common Market have marched together in Europe.

The third change making acceleration possible was in France. The originator of many of the steps toward European integration, France, over the years, had also been in some ways a drag on the process. Though its economy was expanding and its basic productive plant getting stronger, France was continually plagued with inflation and balance of payments difficulties. Domestic politics frustrated efforts to take corrective measures. A strong protectionist tradition was another barrier to trade liberalization. A number of the escape clauses or delaying provisions in the Treaty of Rome were designed with France in mind. The document was full of compromises that were essentially concessions by all the other partners, and especially Germany, to France. One of the largest question marks over the Community at the outset was whether France would be able to live up to its commitments.

An answer came from a surprising source, General de Gaulle, who came to power about six months after the Common Market was established. With a somewhat ambiguous record on European integration, de Gaulle was no champion of the methods and institutions adopted by his predecessors. But the measures he took to put France's economic house in order went far to prepare his country for the challenge of the Common Market.

While it contributed to the acceleration of tariff reduction, the advent of the Fifth Republic brought other uncertainties to the European Community. De Gaulle is no admirer of supranational bodies. *L'Europe des patries* is his formula. Only the nation embodies legitimate political power, in this view, but nations may work closely together and may create international bodies that serve common purposes. While this attitude has undoubtedly had an effect on the distribution of power in the Community, it has not so far been an obstacle to integration. The proposal the Six are now considering for more continuing cooperation in foreign policy stems from France. In January [1962] it was France that forced Germany to choose between accepting some major elements of a common agricultural policy or delaying the passage of the Community into its second stage. Whatever one may think of the economics of this step, it extends the Community and does not delay its realization.

Both these changes in the French position—that helping acceleration of the customs union and that strengthening the intergovernmental element in the Community—have influenced Britain's approach to the Community.

Little Europe got started in 1950 and remained a group of six largely because Britain was not prepared to embark on the course of close integration the others chose. There were many reasons for this. A principal factor was unwillingness to accept supranational institutions and the idea of an eventual United States of Europe. Britain did not want to be enclosed in a purely European organization because of the strain it feared would be placed on Commonwealth ties and its special links with the United States. Economically, the British thought in global terms and felt that throwing in their lot with a purely European group would create problems for their overseas trade and the international position of the pound sterling and the City of London.

BRITAIN AND THE COMMUNITY

As its leading role in the OEEC had demonstrated, Britain was prepared for close economic cooperation with the Continent, but always on terms that permitted London to keep most of its freedom of action in the outside, global economy. A treaty of association with the Coal and Steel Community provided means of dealing with some mutual problems. Some cooperation with Euratom has proved possible, partly through a second international organization under OEEC auspices. It was the Common Market that presented the real problem. If it were realized as planned, Britain would eventually find itself outside a common tariff wall, so that its exports would be handicapped in the major markets of the continent compared with those of France and Germany.

Britain first proposed a free trade area that would include the

Six and the other members of the OEEC. These countries would gradually remove tariffs and quotas on trade in industrial products among themselves. Agricultural trade would be treated separately and each member would keep its own tariff and trade policy in relations with the rest of the world. The EEC would continue to exist but the other members of the free trade area would not make similar commitments to form an economic union. Long negotiations failed.

Technical difficulties played a part in the failure but two other elements were much more important. One was the continental feeling that the proposed bargain was onesided: Britain would get free access to a larger market than it opened to the others, and without undertaking the responsibilities they had agreed to accept. The other was the belief that the future of the Community would be jeopardized if its most concrete immediate benefits were given to a number of other countries that did not join it. The ability of the Community to achieve internal solidarity would be weakened if it had no clear external frontier, so to speak. Also contributing to the failure of the negotiations was the pervasive suspicion that the British really wanted to break up the close cooperation between France and Germany that was at the heart of the Community.

Britain's next step was to join with Denmark, Sweden, Norway, Switzerland, Austria, and Portugal to form the European Free Trade Association (EFTA), a free trade area for manufactured goods, bolstered by bilateral arrangements for certain agricultural products and a few provisions concerning other aspects of cooperation. While EFTA promised some economic benefits for its members it was widely regarded as a move to improve the Outer Seven's chances of striking a bargain with the Six later on. The Community made it clear it was not interested in this approach but would deal singly with any outside country that felt itself hurt by the Common Market or that wished to seek association with it.

The United States made it clear that while it was concerned that the division of Europe into two trading blocs should not weaken the free world politically, it was not prepared to press the Six to negotiate for a free trade area. Washington took the lead in replacing the OEEC with the OECD (Organization for Economic Cooperation and Development), with full American and Canadian membership, and a charter that reduced its functions in matters of intra-

European trade and payments. The decision to accelerate tariff reduction in the EEC and to move faster toward the common external tariff demonstrated the determination of the Six to push ahead with their plan and increased the degree of discrimination against products from outside the area.

The British apparently concluded that they were facing some new facts and that their earlier position would have to be re-examined. In public discussion and inside the government the arguments for and against membership in the EEC were debated while ways were sought of solving the problems Britain was bound to face if it tried to join the Six. The sluggishness of the British economy in contrast to the expansion in Europe, the willingness of British industry to face increased competition, changes in the Commonwealth, and a benevolent American attitude toward the prospect of British membership all went into this calculation. The basic decision, however, must have been taken on the grounds of a fundamental assessment of the future of Britain's political and economic relationship to Europe and to the rest of the world.

EUROPE AND THE U.S.

The ramifications of possible British membership create problems for the United States that are added to the more familiar one of the extension of the area of Europe in which American goods will be at a tariff disadvantage. To deal with some of them President Kennedy has asked for new powers over the tariff. Thus, progress in Europe has forced the United States to face trade policy problems that it has previously managed to push aside. The best course for the United States, if the President is given new powers, is not to follow the British course of joining the Common Market but to work with the enlarged European Community to reduce not only mutual trade barriers but those that harm the interests of the rest of the free world.

Europe's place in the world and Europe's internal problems were mainsprings of the movement for integration. Europe's achievement in making that movement real—even though it still has far to go—combines with the renewed strength of the European economy, to give European integration an increasing impact on the rest of the world.

A FERMENT OF CHANGE

Jean Monnet

Jean Monnet was formerly Commissaire au Plan and President of the High Authority of the European Coal and Steel Community. He is now President of the Action Committee for a United States of Europe. In this article, he describes the setting for the Common Market in terms of the substantial economic, scientific, and political changes that have taken place in the twentieth century. The Common Market is considered a change in itself of considerable proportion. The political and economic necessity which gave birth to the EEC also caused new methods to be developed for common action, namely the institutional approach. Recognizing the need for further development particularly in the political sphere, Monnet suggests that the new power of Europe is much different from the national state of the nineteenth century and can avoid the problems of nationalism.

I

This century has probably changed the manner of life more for every one of us than all the thousands of years of man's progress put together. In the past, men were largely at the mercy of nature. Today, in our industrial countries of the Western world and elsewhere, we are acquiring an unprecedented mastery over nature. Natural resources are no longer a limitation now that we control more and more forms of energy and can use raw materials in more and more ways. We are entering the age of abundance where work, as we know it, will only be one of many human activities. For the first time we in the West are witnessing the emergence of a truly mass society marked by mass consumption, mass education and even mass culture.

"A Ferment of Change" by Jean Monnet from the *Journal of Common Market Studies* (Vol. 1, No. 3). Reprinted by permission of the Journal of Common Market Studies.

We are moving, in the West, from a society where privilege was part of nature to one where the enjoyment of human rights and human dignity are common to all. Unfortunately, two-thirds of mankind have not shared in this process.

And now, on the very eve of creating unprecedented conditions of abundance, we are suddenly faced with the consequences of our extraordinary mastery over the physical forces of nature. Modern medicine is steadily increasing our prospects of life, so that the population of the world is increasing fantastically fast. The United States, which had 76 million people in 1900 and has 180 million today, will probably reach a population of 300 million in the year 2000—a fourfold increase. America can afford this. But we all know what terrible pressures on resources the growth of population is creating in Asia. There, the number of people will have multiplied five times in a century, from 850 million in 1900 to almost 4,000 million in the year 2000. This revolution is creating new explosive pressures of all kinds in the world. At the same time, science is repeatedly creating new powers of destruction. This faces us with the greatest threat humanity has ever had to deal with. The issue today is no longer peace or war, but the triumph or destruction of civilized life.

We cannot assume that we shall avoid such destruction. We have only to look back on the last fifty years to see how constant the risk of upheaval has become. No region of the world has escaped violence. One-third of mankind has become Communist, another third has obtained independence from colonialism, and even among the remaining third nearly all countries have undergone revolutions or wars. True, atomic bombs have made nuclear war so catastrophic that I am convinced no country wishes to resort to it. But I am equally convinced that we are at the mercy of an error of judgment or a technical breakdown, the source of which no man may ever know.

We are then in a world of rapid change, in which men and nations must learn to control themselves in their relations with others. This, to my mind, can only be done through institutions: and it is this need for common institutions that we have learnt in Europe since the war.

II

We are used to thinking that major changes in the traditional relations between countries only take place violently, through conquest or revolution. We are so accustomed to this that we find it hard to appreciate those that are taking place peacefully in Europe even though they have begun to affect the world. We can see the Communist revolution, because it has been violent and because we have been living with it for nearly fifty years. We can see the revolution in the ex-colonial areas because power is plainly changing hands. But we tend to miss the magnitude of the change in Europe because it is taking place by the constitutional and democratic methods which govern our countries.

Yet we have only to look at the difference between 1945 and today to see what an immense transformation has been taking place under our very eyes, here in what used to be called the old world. After the war, the nations of continental Europe were divided and crippled, their national resources were depleted and, in most of them, the peoples had little faith in the future. During the last fifteen years, these countries have lost their empires. It might have been expected they would be further depressed by what many considered the loss of past greatness and prestige.

And yet, after all these upheavals, the countries of continental Europe, which have fought each other so often in the past and which, even in peacetime, organized their economies as potential instruments of war, are now uniting in a Common Market which is laying the foundations for political union. Britain is negotiating to enter this European Community and by this very fact changing the tradition of centuries. And now the President of the United States is already asking Congress for powers to negotiate with the enlarged European Common Market.

To understand this extraordinary change in all its basic simplicity, we must go back to 1950, only five years after the war. For five years, the whole French nation had been making efforts to recreate the bases of production, but it became evident that to go beyond recovery toward steady expansion and higher standards of life for all, the resources of a single nation were not sufficient. It was necessary to transcend the national framework.

The need was political as well as economic. The Europeans had to overcome the mistrust born of centuries of feuds and wars. The governments and peoples of Europe still thought in the old terms of victors and vanquished. Yet, if a basis for peace in the world was to be established, these notions had to be eliminated. Here again, one had to go beyond the nation and the conception of national interest as an end in itself.

We thought that both these objectives could in time be reached if conditions were created enabling these countries to increase their resources by merging them in a large and dynamic common market; and if these same countries could be made to consider that their problems were no longer solely of national concern, but were mutual European responsibilities.

Obviously this could not be done all at once. It was not possible to create a large dynamic market immediately nor to produce trust between recent enemies overnight. After several unsuccessful attempts, the French Government through its Foreign Minister, M. Robert Schuman, proposed in 1950 what many people today would regard as a modest beginning but which seemed very bold at the time: and the Parliaments of France, Germany, Italy, and Benelux voted that, for coal and steel, their countries would form a single common market, run by common institutions administering common rules, very much as within a single nation. The European Coal and Steel Community was set up. In itself this was a technical step, but its new procedures, under common institutions, created a silent revolution in men's minds. It proved decisive in persuading businessmen, civil servants, politicians, and trade unionists that such an approach could work and that the economic and political advantages of unity over division were immense. Once they were convinced, they were ready to take further steps forward.

In 1957, only three years after the failure of the European Army, the six Parliaments ratified the Treaty of Rome which extended the Common Market from coal and steel to an economic union embracing all goods. Today, the Common Market, with its 170 million people that will become 225 million when Britain joins, is creating in Europe a huge continental market on the American scale.

The large market does not prejudge the future economic systems of Europe. Most of the Six have a nationalized sector as large as the

British and some also have planning procedures. These are just as compatible with private enterprise on the large market as they are within a single nation. The contribution of the Common Market is to create new opportunities of expansion for all the members, which make it easier to solve any problems that arise, and to provide the rest of the world with prospects of growing trade that would not exist without it. In Europe, an open society looking to the future is replacing a defensive one regretting the past.

This profound change is being made possible essentially by the new method of common action which is the core of the European Community. To establish this new method of common action, we adapted to our situation the methods which have allowed individuals to live together in society: common rules which each Member is committed to respect, and common institutions to watch over the application of these rules. Nations have applied this method within their frontiers for centuries, but they have never yet been applied between them. After a period of trial and error, this method has become a permanent dialogue between a single European body, responsible for expressing the view of the general interest of the Community and the national governments expressing the national views. The resulting procedure for collective decisions is something quite new and, as far as I know, has no analogy in any traditional system. It is not federal because there is no central government; the nations make their decisions together in the Council of Ministers. On the other hand, the independent European body proposes policies, and the common element is further underlined by the European Parliament and the European Court of Justice.

This system leads to a completely changed approach to common action. In the past, the nations felt no irrevocable commitment. Their responsibility was strictly to themselves, not to any common interest. They had to rely on themselves alone. Relations took the form either of domination if one country was much stronger than the others, or of the trading of advantages if there was a balance of power between them. This balance was necessarily unstable and the concessions made in an agreement one year could always be retracted the next.

But in the European Communities, common rules applied by joint institutions give each a responsibility for the effective working of the Community as a whole. This leads the nations, within the discipline of the Community, to seek a solution to the problems themselves, instead of trading temporary advantages. It is this method which explains the dramatic change in the relations of Germany with France and the other Common Market countries. Looking forward to a common future has made them agree to live down the feuds of the past. Today people have almost forgotten that the Saar was ever a problem and yet from 1919 to 1950 it was a major bone of contention between France and Germany. European unity has made it seem an anachronism. And today, at French invitation, German troops are training on French soil.

So the progress toward unity is well on its way. But before we turn to wider issues beyond Europe there are two further problems to be examined within Europe itself.

III

Firstly, we must bear in mind that economic integration cannot yield its full fruit unless our countries step up their present efforts and quickly stop the waste of intelligence among their young people by making access to higher education truly democratic. Of course there has been progress in this field, but it has been too little and too slow. Now we must set out on an energetic European campaign which must speedily change the conditions under which higher education is available to the youth of our countries. We cannot judge our education simply by its intellectual level. How can one fail to be struck by the fact that, with roughly equal populations, the United States has 3 million students, the Soviet Union 2 million, and the Community of the Six only 600,000? Contrary to what we might think about the development of education in our countries with their older civilizations, secondary and higher education are very limited in Europe compared with these two great new countries. Today what divides men most is not money but education. One might hazard the estimate that in the Community more than 50 per cent of the children of workers and peasants never receive any general education beyond the primary school level. Eight out of ten children whose parents are in responsible positions go to secondary schools which open up the normal path to higher education, while scarcely two out of ten children of workers and peasants have this opportunity.

The economic integration of Europe in the Common Market will give us resources we now lack, and which should allow us to extend to all our citizens the benefits of higher education. This will permit them to make their full contribution to the progress of the Community and at the same time benefit from it to the full in their personal lives.

IV

Beyond the economic integration of our countries and the increase in our wealth which it will bring there remains the problem of achieving our political union which was our aim from the beginning. As you know, I have always felt that the political union of Europe must be built step by step like its economic integration. One day this process will then lead us to a European Federation.

At the point which we have now reached, many are asking themselves whether Britain's entry into the Common Market will not put a brake on our efforts of economic integration and would not compromise the political unity of our countries. But I do not share these fears. I am convinced that the British today are anxious to enter the European Community, not simply in order to take part in its economic growth, but also because they are necessarily conscious that none of our countries can any longer separately exercise any real influence in world affairs, and that only the union of Europe whose fate they wish to share will allow them to exercise this necessary political influence.

Entering the Common Market will inevitably change the behavior of Britain as it has changed that of each of our Six countries. When Britain is a member she will wish to contribute to the success of a Community which will then be hers just as much as it is now ours. The days are past when we debated the pros and cons of the little and the big Europe, of integration versus cooperation: Europe with its rules and its institutions will be the framework in which our countries will express their energies in common within a single Community. That is why I believe that the prospect of Britain's entry has not only an economic significance, but is a historical polit ical event, and why we must all make every effort that the negotiations between the Six and Britain should quickly succeed.

V

We have seen that Europe has overcome the attitude of domination which ruled state policies for so many centuries. But quite apart from what this means for us in the old continent, this is a fact of world importance. It is obvious that countries and peoples who are overcoming this state of mind between themselves will bring the same mentality to their relations with others, outside Europe. The new method of action developed in Europe replaces the efforts at domination of nation states by a constant process of collective adaptation to new conditions, a chain reaction, a ferment where one change induces another.

Look at the effect the Common Market has already had on world tariffs. When it was set up, it was widely assumed the member countries would want to protect themselves and become, as some put it, an inward-looking group. Yet everything that has happened since has shown this view to be wrong. The Six have reduced the tariffs among themselves and toward other countries faster than expected. Now President Kennedy proposes America and Europe should cut tariffs on manufactures by half, and the Common Market will certainly welcome it. This leads to a situation where tariffs throughout the major trading areas of the world will be lower than they have ever been.

These changes inside and outside Europe would not have taken place without the driving force of the Common Market. It opens new prospects for dealing with problems the solution of which was becoming increasingly urgent. I am thinking of world agriculture in a more and more industrial civilization; of links between the new and the long-established industrial regions, and in particular of the need for growing trade between Japan and the United States and Europe together.

Naturally, increasing trade will also benefit the Commonwealth. The prospect of Britain's future entry into the Common Market has already made the Continent more aware than ever before of the problems of the Commonwealth. Clearly, for countries whose major need is to obtain more capital for development, the fact that Britain is part of a rapidly developing Europe holds great promise of future progress.

Similarly, problems are arising that only Europe and the United States together have the resources to deal with. The need to develop policies of sustained growth, which in large part depend on maintaining international monetary stability, is an example. Increasing the aid of the West to the under-developed areas on a large scale is another. Separately, the European nations have inevitably taken divergent views of aid policies. But tomorrow, the nations of Europe by acting together can make a decisive contribution. The necessary precondition of such a partnership between America and Europe is that Europe should be united and thus be able to deploy resources on the same scale as America. This is what is in the course of happening today.

That we have begun to cooperate on these affairs at the Atlantic level is a great step forward. It is evident that we must soon go a good deal further toward an Atlantic Community. The creation of a united Europe brings this nearer by making it possible for America and Europe to act as partners on an equal footing. I am convinced that ultimately, the United States too will delegate powers of effective action to common institutions, even on political questions. Just as the United States in their own day found it necessary to unite, just as Europe is now in the process of uniting, so the West must move toward some kind of union. This is not an end in itself. It is the beginning on the road to the more orderly world we must have if we are to escape destruction.

The discussions on peace today are dominated by the question of disarmament. The world will be more and more threatened by destruction as long as bombs continue to pile up on both sides. Many therefore feel that the hopes for peace in the world depend on as early an agreement on armaments as possible, particularly an agreement on nuclear arms. Of course we must continue to negotiate on these questions. But it is too simple to hope the problems that arise out of philosophic conflicts could be settled without a change in the view which people take of the future. For what is the Soviet objective? It is to achieve a Communist world, as Mr. Kruschev has told us many times. When this becomes so obviously impossible that nobody, even within a closed society, can any longer believe it—when the partnership of America and a United Europe makes it plain to all that the West may change from within but that others cannot change it by outside pressures, then Mr. Kruschev or his successor will accept the facts, and the conditions will at last exist for turning so-called peaceful coexistence into genuine peace. Then at last real disarmament will become possible.

Personally, I do not think we shall have to wait long for this change. The history of European unification shows that when people become convinced a change is taking place that creates a new situation, they act on their revised estimate before that situation is established. After all, Britain has asked to join the Common Market before it was complete. The President of the United States is seeking powers to negotiate with the European Community on steps to an Atlantic partnership even before Britain has joined. Can we not expect a similar phenomenon in the future relations with the Soviet Union?

VI

What conclusions can we draw from all these thoughts?

One impression predominates in my mind over all others. It is this: unity in Europe does not create a new kind of great power; it is a method for introducing change in Europe and consequently in the world. People, more often outside the European Community than within, are tempted to see the European Community as a potential nineteenth-century state with all the overtones of power this implies. But we are not in the nineteenth century, and the Europeans have built up the European Community precisely in order to find a way out of the conflicts to which the nineteenth-century power philosophy gave rise. The natural attitude of a European Community based on the exercise by nations of common responsibilities will be to make these nations also aware of their responsibilities, as a Community, to the world. In fact, we already see this sense of world responsibilities developing as unity in Europe begins to affect Britain, America, and many other areas of the world. European unity is not a blueprint, it is not a theory, it is a process that has already begun, of bringing peoples and nations together to adapt themselves jointly to changing circumstances.

European unity is the most important event in the West since the war, not because it is a new great power, but because the new institutional method it introduces is permanently modifying relations between nations and men. Human nature does not change, but when nations and men accept the same rules and the same institutions to make sure that they are applied, their behavior toward each other changes. This is the process of civilization itself.

NATO AND THE EUROPEAN
ECONOMIC COMMUNITY

Walter Hallstein

*Walter Hallstein is the President of the Commission of the Euro-
pean Economic Community. This article was adapted from an address given at a meeting of NATO Parliamentarians on November
12, 1962. Professor Hallstein discusses the economic and political
goals of the Common Market and thereby indicates the vision of
progress that make the integration effort worthwhile. He looks beyond developments in Europe and sees a working partnership beginning between the new Europe and the United States. He then turns
to discuss NATO, the military aspect of the Atlantic Alliance. He
analyzes the two major questions of NATO: how to spread responsibility more evenly and how to increase mutual trust, and then
looks to the future Atlantic partnership.*

The European Economic Community is still a very young multinational institution. At the time it started operations—January 1,
1958—some feared it, some doubted that it would succeed. Today,
the Community is an accepted fact: it has proved itself, and it has
proved itself liberal. Great Britain and other European countries are
seeking to join it or associate themselves with it; Greece, cradle of
European civilization, has become an associate and may in the near
future become a member of the EEC. In a word, the European scene
is being transformed.

I

The birth of the Community coincided roughly with the passing
of one particular phase of postwar history—the phase of European
recovery, associated with Marshall Plan aid and with the Organization for European Economic Cooperation (OEEC). Today, the

"NATO and the European Economic Community" by Walter Hallstein from
Orbis (Vol. VI, No. 4, January 1963, published by the Foreign Policy Research
Institute, University of Pennsylvania). Reprinted by permission of Orbis.

OEEC has been replaced by the OECD (Organization for Economic Cooperation and Development)—an Atlantic organization to take the place of a purely European one. If the European scene is being transformed, so is the Atlantic scene; and President Kennedy's Trade Expansion Act marks a further stage in that transformation. Together, we stand at the threshold of a new era, the era of Atlantic Partnership.

These two great transformations did not coincide by accident. Each is partly the cause of the other, and partly the effect. In 1959, an official of the Community would have found it necessary to explain and, indeed, to defend the European Community. He would have spoken not as a German, or a Frenchman, or Belgian, but as a European citizen with European responsibilities. Today, the same official would speak not only as a European, but also as an Atlantic citizen—to try to set forth how his colleagues see their Atlantic responsibilities, within the double framework of the Alliance that already is and the Partnership that is to be.

There is also a third change that has now occurred. Quite recently, the Soviet Union began to show new interest in the growing European Community. From the beginning, of course, the Community has been the target of what seemed to be routine propaganda attacks. What is new is that these attacks have now become more serious, more subtle, and more sustained. Only last spring, we were made aware of Premier Khrushchev's personal attention. The Common Market, he said, "is a state monopoly agreement of the financial oligarchy of Western Europe which the aggressive quarters of imperialism use with the object of strengthening NATO and stepping up the arms race." It was paradoxical, to say the least, that at about the same time some of the Community's friends and allies were pondering the same problem, asking themselves how a united Europe could best be fitted into the Atlantic framework, while others were voicing their anxiety lest Europe be tempted by the old mirage of a so-called "third force."

Obviously, such conflicting theories cannot both be right. Indeed, they are both wrong. But the question remains, what in fact—not in fear or fancy—is the European Community; and what is its place in the great forum of freedom?

II

First, what is the Community, or rather, what is it becoming? For it is a process, not a product. Indeed, it has been well said that the EEC is a kind of peaceful three-stage rocket. The first stage is that of the customs union; the second, economic union; and the third, political union. Today, the Community is nearly halfway toward a full customs union; it has embarked, decisively, on economic union, and it is already clear how deeply the implications of political union are embedded in the other two.

Already, tariffs on industrial goods traded among the Community's member states have been cut by half—eighteen months ahead of schedule. Those on an agreed list of farm products have been cut by 35 per cent—again ahead of schedule. By next July [1963], the EEC will have completed two-thirds of the process of leveling off the member states' external tariffs into the Community's single tariff, itself already reduced by the "Dillon round" of negotiations with our partners in the rest of the Free World. In this last respect, the EEC will then be two-and-a-half years ahead of schedule; and the Commission of the EEC proposed at the end of October 1962 that the full customs union should be completed by 1967—a full three years ahead of schedule.

At the beginning of 1962, moreover, an equally significant landmark was sighted and passed. Painfully, arduously, but triumphantly, the Community moved into the second four-year stage of the transition period under the Treaty of Rome. From now on, only a proposal from the Commission can delay the transition period, and then only if such a proposal is accepted by all member states. As of now, majority voting, which has already been applied in the Community's Council of Ministers on a number of issues, is automatically extended to a number of others—a symbol, as well as an instrument, of our growing unity.

Our passage into Stage Two symbolized also the fact that the economic union has already begun. The first moves have been made to liberalize the movement of capital and persons; the first forms of national discrimination in transportation have been removed. The first antitrust regulations are being applied: so far some 800 agreements among three or more firms have been selected for screening by the Commission. More important still, the EEC made a beginning upon common policies in the three key fields marked out by our founding Treaty—agriculture, transportation and foreign trade. Moreover, less spectacular but equally vital work is now going forward in innumerable other spheres of the Community's unifying activity, on labor programs, patents, tax systems, monetary problems, and the harmonization of countless national laws.

In this connection, a few figures will indicate the way things have been developing. Of course, nobody can offer mathematical proof that this progress is attributable to the European Economic Community alone; but it is reasonable to assert that this progress would not have been possible had there been no Common Market. For example, the gross product of the Community increased by 24 per cent between 1958 and 1961. Industrial production alone went up 29 per cent, while trade between Community countries rose by 73 per cent. Its external trade also showed a considerable rise in this period of 27 per cent. This is greater than the general expansion of world trade, which was only 19 per cent. These figures should suffice to give an idea of the dynamic way in which the Community is developing.

What is emerging from all this is not just an economic union. Rather, it is a political union, thus far limited to the economic and social fields. It is because this union is political, indeed, that the Commission recently put forward a comprehensive action program intended to fill out with flesh and blood the bare bones of the Treaty: the completion of the "European constitution" with "European laws" is too great a matter to be left to chance.

How soon that constitution may be extended to new fields—culture, defense, foreign affairs (other than commercial policy which is already covered by the Treaty)—remains an open question; so too does the precise form that such extension may take. This form might be modeled on the existing constitutional mechanism, the Community's institutions; on the other hand, it may be that for the time being other forms of unity will have to be sought. But certainly the existing mechanism must and will continue to function, and its essential principle—that of a Community element which is more

than the sum of the national parts—should have a place in whatever
new mechanism may be created in the future.

Such, then, is the developing European Community—a new fact,
a new force, and a new friend for its allies and partners. What is
the response of other Atlantic friends to this new phenomenon?
How can we understand each other, face each other's problems, live
together, work and trade and strive together? The answer is insep-
arably linked with the development of United States policy toward
Europe since the war.

III

From the very beginning of the postwar period, America has
steadfastly supported the unification of Europe. The same basic
theme has run through four administrations, two of them Democratic, two of them Republican. It is continuous from 1947, when
Secretary of State George C. Marshall expressed the then distant
hope that the "logic of history" would draw Europe together "not
only for its own survival but for the stability, prosperity, and peace
of the entire world." It found a fresh echo in 1962, when President
John F. Kennedy reaffirmed that the United States looked on the
"vast new enterprise" of the European Community "with hope and
admiration," and declared: "We do not regard a strong and united
Europe as a rival, but as a partner."

The OEEC and NATO were the first organic expressions of this
Atlantic solidarity. The OEEC, offspring and distributor of Marshall
Plan aid, can now be seen as a kind of American and Canadian
"self-denying ordinance," allowing to a ruined and impoverished
Europe economic and commercial privileges which gave her a
breathing-space for her postwar recovery. But the very success of
the OEEC and the European Payments Union in liberalizing intra-
European trade and payments was at length to remove the *raison
d'être* of this privileged position. With the consequent disappearance
of discrimination against the dollar, there remained to the OEEC
only its third main function—intra-European cooperation in matters
of economic policy. It would be idle as well as unfair to deny the
usefulness of such cooperation, but as a basis for unity in Europe it

was gravely weakened by the looseness of its framework. As a basis for Atlantic partnership it was weaker still, not only because the United States and Canada had merely the status of observers in the OEEC, but more especially because within it the separate nations of Europe were insufficiently united to speak with their transatlantic partners on equal terms.

The formation of NATO expressed a different kind of Atlantic solidarity. Its basic logic—common defense against possible aggression—is that of a classical defensive alliance; so, in many respects, is its formal structure. But because one of its members is immeasurably more powerful than any of the others, it has always demanded from that member the highest degree of responsibility, and from the others the highest degree of trust. That responsibility has never faltered; but the need for it, and the complementary need for trust in it, are magnified a thousandfold by the conditions of thermonuclear warfare. Small wonder, indeed, that the Atlantic Alliance has been continually subject to stresses and strains.

This is not the place to recall past difficulties. Suffice it to say that the specific and immediate causes of stress and strain have been manifold, including NATO members' other commitments, recurrent balance-of-payments problems, political, and strategic debates, questions of atomic secrecy, and the continual, inevitable tension between the need for a plausible deterrent and the fear of its being unleashed except as a very last resort.

Of course, the most radical solution to all these problems—as indeed to so many of the fears and tensions that beset our world—is controlled disarmament in both the nuclear and the conventional spheres. Toward this goal we must and shall continue to strive. But until we have attained it we must face facts, those somber facts that make our military alliance a vital guarantee of peace. How then can we improve its workings?

Over the past thirteen-and-a-half years the Atlantic Alliance has proved its flexibility by continually adjusting to new situations and new developments in military technology. Various attempts have been made, sometimes successfully, to palliate the immediate causes of stress and strain. But the basic structure of the Alliance, with its twin and complementary demands for responsibility on the one hand and trust on the other, has remained unchanged. Essentially, the problem has been twofold: how to spread the responsibility more evenly, and how at the same time to increase mutual trust.

These are highly controversial matters which need not concern us here—controversies that still surround the question of independent deterrents, the proliferation of nuclear weapons, and the more technical but no less hotly debated problems of military division of labor, tactical nuclear weapons, the "escalation" theory, and the so-called "permissive link" system. However, the creation of a united Europe potentially affects both aspects of the basic problem, responsibility and trust.

Of the former it may still be premature to speak, but two facts might profitably be recalled. The first is that in the days of the European Defense Community project there was no question of its "dividing NATO"; the United States strongly supported the project precisely as a step toward spreading the responsibility for common defense more evenly throughout the Alliance. This, it is true, was in the non-nuclear field. But the second fact qualifies the preceding statement: it is the remark made by Presidential Assistant McGeorge Bundy in his now celebrated speech in Copenhagen in September 1962. He said that no one should suppose that the United States is unwilling to share in this grim responsibility whenever the responsibility was truly shared. It would also be wrong, he added, to suppose that the reluctance which the U.S. feels with respect to individual forces would extend automatically to a European force, genuinely unified and multilateral, and effectively integrated with the necessarily predominant strength of the United States in the whole nuclear defense of the Alliance.

IV

Now let us turn to the second aspect of the twin problem—the question of mutual trust. NATO has always sought to be more than a merely military alliance. Article 2 of the North Atlantic Treaty calls for economic collaboration, and Article 4 for political consultation. In 1956 the Committee of Three recommended, and the NATO Council established, institutions to serve these ends. This, perhaps, was a first attempt to set up what might be called the intrastructure for greater mutual trust—a first attempt, in fact, at Atlantic Partnership in the nonmilitary field. That such an attempt was urgently necessary became more apparent as the deterrent was seen to be effective: short of war, it was vital to be able to meet aggression on the economic and political level. And yet, looking at the fruits of NATO's economic and political efforts, who can feel satisfied that true Atlantic Partnership has been established?

To say this is not to criticize the dedication and the skill of those who have worked, and are still working, to further the economic and political efforts of NATO. The root cause lies deeper. It, too, is inherent in the structure of the Alliance, grouping as it originally did one giant member and fourteen others each of whom is inevitably smaller than a world power of continental size. Partnership, in fact, is only possible between comparative equals.

The decisive change that has now transformed this situation is the establishment of the European Community. The Community has a long way to go before it is ready in all fields to be a full and equal partner of the United States. But already the creation of the European Community has had two Atlantic consequences, both of them positive, neither of them divisive.

The first is the transformation of the OEEC into the OECD. In the new organization, the United States and Canada are full members, not just observers: hence the word "European" has been dropped from its title. Furthermore, its purpose is no longer the recovery of Europe, but the development of the Free World: hence the word "Development" has been added.

The second consequence of the creation of the European Community is no less significant. That is the bold and imaginative Trade Expansion Act recently passed by the United States Congress and specifically designed by President Kennedy to meet the challenge and opportunity presented in the first instance by the European Community. Under the new act, the President is empowered to make greater tariff reductions—even to the point of eliminating certain tariffs—and to negotiate in broad categories of goods rather than by the cumbersome item-by-item system of the past. Equally important is the provision in the act for trade adjustment assistance to American firms and workers adversely affected by increased imports, a pledge that what is in prospect is a serious attempt at trade partnership, not just an exercise of tariff-cutting where it hurts—and matters—least.

In these two ways, then, partnership is in prospect. What, in concrete terms, does this mean here and now? In this connection it is well to define our terms. Thus far, we have employed the term "Atlantic Partnership," not "Atlantic Community." The term "Atlantic Community" should be rejected in order to avoid misunderstanding. In the sense that we are now accustomed to use it, the word "Community" implies an innovation, adopted to describe the fundamentally new organism established by the Treaties of Paris and Rome. If that organism is not fully either a federation or a confederation, it is nevertheless very different from even such an international organization as NATO. It certainly has federal elements, involves what Prime Minister Harold Macmillan has aptly termed "the pooling of sovereignty," and already represents partial political union. Would it be reasonable, then, to expect the United States to join in so thoroughgoing a venture? Would it even be conceivable? Most Americans will agree that American public opinion is a very long way from accepting such an idea.

Nor is this a question that concerns the United States alone. Even if American public opinion were by some miracle to accept the idea of the United States "joining the European Community," thus transforming it into "an Atlantic Community," it is very unlikely to be feasible in practice. So vast a geographical extension of the Community would wreck the whole operation.

❖   ❖   ❖

VI

One need not be pessimistic about the future. Certainly there are tasks facing the future Atlantic Partnership; these must be explored. First in line are the trade negotiations, which have to be prepared and studied not merely for their commercial consequences, to see that the balance is even, but also for their deeper economic meaning. How far, for example, shall we have to envisage, within the Atlantic Partnership, something of the harmonization of economic conditions—on both sides, and in the interests of both partners—that is already necessary within the European Community? How can we so steer the negotiations that they benefit not only the two major partners, but the Atlantic world and the Free World as a whole?

Then there is the question of world agriculture. Already, under the spur of the British negotiations, we envisage world commodity agreements. What role can the Atlantic Partnership play in their organization? What precisely should be their content? How shall their obvious dangers be avoided? How can they be linked with the concomitant questions of aid?

Wherever one looks, indeed, one sees vast challenges. There is the world monetary problem: how can the European Community, how can the Atlantic Partnership safeguard the fruits of men's labor and their thrift? There is the problem of the so-called terms of trade: how can Europe and America, with our wealth and our consequent responsibility, face the double dilemma of maintaining our own stability without progressively mulcting those less fortunate than we? There is the problem of booms and slumps: can our joint ingenuity devise methods of meeting them without any longer merely exporting our problems until they return to plague us, multiplied by our partners' problems too?

These are some of our tasks. We have the means to tackle them. But we should not rush to set up some central Atlantic body to direct our efforts. First of all, a major part of those efforts, paradoxical as it may seem, must continue to be competitive. We must harness the forces of free competition, curbing their ill effects, as the European Community has done. Part of the purpose of tariff-cutting, indeed, is to set these expansionist forces free. But there is a second reason for distrust of a priori institutions. As yet, we do not know what precise role they should fulfill. When we do, it will be easier to devise them; but to do so now would involve us all in the sterile discussion of constitutional principles and the meaningless dispute of as yet nonexistent powers. Already, there are four great institutions: NATO, OECD, IMF, and GATT. Let us trust to our collective skill to use them wisely.

To say this is not a counsel of despair. No one can claim that we have found the perfect framework for Atlantic partnership, that these institutions may not need reforming, that their methods may not be improved. But the impulse for reform and improvement is already there. A major part of that impulse and a major part of the new opportunities which we now enjoy derive from the dynamics of European integration, at present limited to economic subject matter, but potentially a major political contribution to the strength of the Free World. That, not a common stake in "imperialism" as Premier Khrushchev alleges, is the true link between the EEC and NATO.

PART II

Consequences of the Common Market

THE CONSEQUENCES FOR ECONOMIC
PLANNING OF JOINING THE COMMON MARKET

A. C. L. Day

Professor A. C. L. Day is Reader in Economics at the London School of Economics. He has written numerous articles and books on various economic subjects. He is well known in the United States and has given testimony to the Joint Economic Committee of the United States Congress. In this article, Professor Day addresses himself to the question of the consequences on economic planning of joining the Common Market. The problem arises because of the obligations associated with being a member and because the Community itself will exercise some economic planning. He examines the different types of economic planning and indicates how each would be effected. When the fixity of exchange rates is recognized, the conclusion is reached that many possible outcomes are conceivable, but that an integration of national policies would probably result.

It is inevitable that membership in the European Economic Community will deprive the individual members, to an increasing extent over time, of their freedom to plan their economies in some of the ways which they might otherwise choose. This, indeed, is an unavoidable counterpart to the fact that the Community is itself an

"The Consequences for Economic Planning of Joining the Common Market" by A. C. L. Day from *The Political Quarterly* (January-March 1963). Reprinted by permission of the Political Quarterly.

institution which is designed to plan and organize certain major features of the economic situation. It is unacceptable that two different bodies—the national state and the Community as a whole— should attempt to plan in contradictory ways, and membership of the Community must, in this sense, involve a substantial abandonment of national sovereignty. At the same time, membership of the Community in no sense implies that the members are committed to a *laissez-faire* free enterprise economy; the whole conception of the Community is one of a mixed economy of the type which was firmly established in Britain in the early postwar years and which is to be found (with varying proportions of planning and *laissez-faire* in the mixture) in all the economically advanced Western countries.

There are two main difficulties in trying to answer the questions to what extent membership of the Community would inhibit a (British) Government's freedom to plan the economy. One difficulty is that it is by no means easy to define what is meant by "planning"; it is one of those words which are used, frequently with a considerable emotional content, but also with little in the way of accurate definition of what is meant. The second difficulty is that the Community is a rapidly evolving institution; it is not difficult to identify the limitations on freedom to plan which are inherent in the Rome Treaty and subsequent Regulations which have been published, but it is impossible to be dogmatic about the further limitations which will appear as the Community evolves. There is an important body of opinion in Europe, which is strongly represented at the Commission in Brussels, which believes that the Community should and must develop into a federal United States of Europe, in which the power of the members would be reduced to something similar to that of states in the United States of America. Whether events do develop in that way or not depends on how political forces work out, and in particular on the will of the national governments making up the Community, which in turn will be largely influenced by the desires of the electorates.

For the present purpose, it is convenient to consider four different ways in which a governmental authority (whether it be a central or local government or an institution such as the European Commission) can plan. It is possible to plan by confrontation, by co-ordination, by prohibition or by active initiation.

PLANNING BY CONFRONTATION

Planning by confrontation occurs when a number of separate bodies (such as all the major firms in an industry, all the governments in a group of countries, or the government and the major industrial firms in a single country) get together to discuss their expectations about the future and the plans that they, individually, are making for the future. Such confrontation has been of some importance in international economic policy in Europe since the war, in the procedures of OEEC and, more recently, OECD. Representatives of national governments and the international secretariat meet together from time to time to discuss what they expect to happen to their national economies and (in broad terms) what they intend to do to correct undesirable developments. In this procedure, if events or policies in one country are likely to have adverse effects on another, then attempts are made by persuasion to do something about it.

To a large extent, the much-praised French domestic planning of the postwar years has relied on a more closely articulated version of such a confrontation procedure. Representatives of major industries and the Government meet (largely by personal contacts in an old-boy network) to inform one another about their expectation and plans for a period of years ahead. In this way, it is possible for the plans of individual industries to be consistent with one another, and with whatever broad developments the Government expects for the economy as a whole, so avoiding waste caused by building unnecessary capacity in one industry and also avoiding bottlenecks through the existence of inadequate capacity in another.

Although it remains unclear how Britain's National Economic Development Council will work out in practice, it is clearly going to be concerned largely with such planning by confrontation. There can be little doubt that such planning is valuable. It allows individual plans (as for plant expansion) to be based on fuller information and therefore to be more rational. It also makes it more possible to identify particular difficulties (e.g. shortage of skilled labor) and so prepares the ground for doing something about them. At the same time, there are real dangers in long-term planning of this kind, because no one can make confident and satisfactory long-term economic predictions on many critical matters—as can be seen, for example, from the stupendous failures of British forecasts of demand and supply of various fuels which have been made since the war. But in spite of the danger that confrontation procedure may lead to everyone acting on the wrong predictions, such planning, used with circumspection, has its value. It will play a big part in the work of the Community, and in the Commission's Report to the Council of Ministers at the end of October 1962, a firm recommendation was made that there should be such a confrontation of the expectations of the Community's members for a five-year period ahead. At worst, such an exercise will be no more than a waste of a good number of committee hours (as may happen if the "predictions" are simply glib extrapolations of past trends). At best, it will provide better information on which to identify particular problems and on which to base a more consistent set of particular plans by individual governments, industries, and firms.

PLANNING BY CO-ORDINATION

The second type of planning listed above—planning by co-ordination—goes beyond planning by confrontation in that the planning body takes a more active role. It acts in such a way as to alter the economic environment in which other decision-making bodies themselves operate. Perhaps the most familiar form is that of changing taxes, either to influence the general level of activity (the now well-established Keynesian techniques) or to influence activity in particular sectors of the economy (such as the reduction in purchase tax on cars, designed to stimulate that particular industry). The other main method of planning by co-ordination is the use of monetary measures, such as changes in interest rates and in the availability of bank credit.

There can be no doubt that planning by co-ordination of this type will continue to play a major role when the Community is fully operative, both in controlling the whole economy (to achieve some politically satisfactory compromise between excessive unemployment and excessive inflation, and to achieve a satisfactory balance of payments situation), and also in influencing particular sectors of the economy. But the major question of how these planning functions will be split between the Community's organs and the national governments is one on which there is still a good deal of ground for uncertainty.

PLANNING BY PROHIBITION

Before proceeding to a consideration of the major issue of how this planning by co-ordination is likely to operate, it will, however, be convenient to consider the two other broad categories of planning which were listed above. The third of them is planning by prohibition—the sort of planning which was common throughout Europe in the early post-war years and which is a considerable part of the armory of controls of even the most *laissez-faire* governments. There is one important kind of planning by prohibition which will become quite impossible once the transition period is over and which, even during the transition period, can only be used to a very limited extent and in quite exceptional circumstances. This is the imposition of import restrictions. If a single country in the Community were to impose such restrictions, it would be acting in a manner directly contrary to the whole purpose of the Rome Treaty. This weapon—one of the most powerful in the armories of controls used by countries in the early postwar years—will be completely unavailable to any member of the Community. Moreover, the power to impose restrictions over capital movements is to be severely limited, although under the First Directive it is still open to members to impose restrictions over short-term capital movements, which are the movements likely to be the most violent and disturbing in an economic or political crisis. These limits to the power to impose planning by prohibition of external transactions undoubtedly impose substantial restraints on national freedom of action, and to that extent they mean that the problems of achieving planning by co-ordination (notably the use of fiscal and monetary policy) are so much the greater.

At the same time, it must be emphasised that there is a great deal of domestic planning by prohibition which can continue unaffected by membership of the Community. For example, town and country planning legislation, building controls and licensing, and prohibition of certain kinds of investment are examples of forms of planning by prohibition which are perfectly permissible under the Treaty.

PLANNING BY ACTIVE INITIATION

The fourth kind of planning listed above is planning by active initiation on the part of a governmental or other authority. Such planning occurs when the government itself goes out and does something—planning the location of industry by subsidizing industry in certain regions or planning the transport system by spending money on new roads or by subsidizing a nationalized railway system. Here, again, the Rome Treaty does impose substantial limits on the freedom of action of governments; Article 92 provides that except where otherwise provided for, state aid "which distorts or threatens to distort competition by favoring certain undertakings or the production of certain goods shall, in so far as it adversely affects trade between Member States, be deemed to be incompatible with the Common Market." The Article then goes on to define those categories of aid which shall be allowed, in spite of this general provision; the important category which is always permitted is "aid having a social character, granted to individual consumers," provided there is no discrimination by origin of the products concerned. The government can give babies black-currant juice, as long as it does not discriminate between English and Italian juice.

More important, there are certain kinds of state aid which may be permissible. They include aid to promote the economic development of regions "where the standard of living is abnormally low or where there is serious under-employment" and aid "intended to facilitate the development of certain activities or certain economic regions, provided that such aid does not adversely affect trading conditions to such an extent as would be contrary to the common interest." In other words, economic planning to help Scotland or Northern Ireland by subsidies has every chance of approval in the Common Market. But in general, subsidies to particular industries or particular lines of activity may have to be justified, by proving that they do not adversely affect trading conditions to an extent contrary to the general interest. Moreover, it is possible that the word "aid" referred to in Article 92 may be interpreted more widely than direct money subsidies and include aid through remission of taxation.

It seems, therefore, that the Treaty will impose some restriction on the power of individual states to plan by active intervention. On the other hand, there is no prohibition whatsoever of intervention by nationalization, although it is worth bearing in mind that the Rome Treaty rules may well prohibit some of the commercial practices of British nationalized industries, such as differential pricing of coal in home and overseas markets and non-publication of specially negotiated railway rates.

MONETARY AND FISCAL POLICIES

The major question which remains to be discussed is the way in which monetary and fiscal policies can be used by members of the Community in order to plan their economies to achieve full employment, price stability, balance-of-payments stability, and a satisfactory rate of economic growth. A reading of the relevant articles of the Treaty would suggest that, in these respects, there will be remarkably little practical restraint on the freedom of action of the members. On the other hand, most of the officials at Brussels and most of the more ardent Continental supporters of the Community (along, let it be said, with some of the more ardent British opponents) consider that the Community must inevitably move toward a common monetary policy and a common currency, and toward a common fiscal policy. This opinion has had its clearest reflection yet in the Report to the Council by the Commission in October 1962. Neither of these two extreme positions should be taken at its face value: the Community is an evolving institution and it is impossible to consider that its final form will be limited to the structure agreed in the Rome Treaty; but at the same time the Commission is a body with a strong interest in obtaining additional powers for itself, and much the best way of achieving a huge increase in its powers is to persuade the members (and prospective members) of the Community that economic policy cannot operate satisfactorily without a great deal of centralization of fiscal and monetary policy.

The fundamental logical problem that arises here has been described on many occasions* and need not detain us for long here. It can be exemplified by describing two extreme approaches to the co-ordination of economic policies of different countries within a common market—i.e., within a group of countries with a common external commercial policy, no trading barriers, and with relatively free internal movement of labor and capital.

At one extreme, there is the solution of complete fiscal and monetary integration, as found in the relations of England and Scotland within the United Kingdom. At the other extreme, there is the solution which gives the biggest possible degree of autonomy to the individual countries, which is consistent with the existence of a "common market" as defined above. This solution is that of allowing fiscal and monetary autonomy, including the power to fix taxes at whatever levels seem appropriate, to have an independent policy on interest rates, and (the fundamental point) the power to vary the exchange rate between one's own currency and that of the other members of the common market.

If effective freedom to run one's own monetary and fiscal policy is to be maintained, then the freedom to alter exchange rates is the only way available to be certain of maintaining the common market. For example, if a country decides (perhaps for reasons of income distribution) to maintain low interest rates relative to those of its colleagues in the common market, the effect is likely to be a net outflow of capital, which weakens its balance of payments. Again, if it decides to follow a fiscal policy leading to particularly low levels of unemployment relatively to its colleagues, it is likely to cause faster inflation than in its colleagues, and its goods are likely to be less competitive—and so again it finds itself with a weaker balance of payments. Again, if it is a country with a shortage of innovating entrepreneurs, a conservative labor force, a remoteness from the main market areas, or a rather unfavorable geographical endowment of raw materials, then its goods are likely to become relatively less competitive with its colleagues in a common market, which is likely to lead in turn to relatively heavy unemployment and to balance-of-payments difficulties—and if it tries to deal with the

* A good recent discussion is in J. J. Polak: *International Co-ordination of Economic Policy*, International Monetary Fund Staff Papers, July 1962,

unemployment by expansionary domestic, fiscal, or monetary policies, it in turn finds itself with all the more serious balance of payments problems. The upshot is that it is always possible that policies or circumstances may lead a country with an independent fiscal and monetary policy into payments difficulties. For a time, it can deal with these difficulties by drawing on reserves—but they are exhaustible and cannot be used indefinitely. Sooner or later, it must abandon its independence, or make its goods more competitive by altering the exchange rate, since it would be quite inconsistent with the ground rules of a common market to impose its own private import restrictions. At the one extreme, full fiscal and monetary independence within a common market implies full freedom to alter the exchange rate.

At the other extreme, an immutably fixed exchange rate (as presumably can be taken to exist between England and Scotland) implies that, within a common market, a country cannot maintain any substantial degree of independence in its fiscal and monetary policies. There can, indeed, be a little; for example individual states in the United States have different local income taxes, and on rare occasions, different regions in the Federal Reserve System have followed slightly different interest rate policies. But in comparison with the degree of national autonomy to which we have become accustomed in modern nation states, it can safely be said that a common market with immutably fixed exchange rates would deprive member states of much the greater part of their fiscal and monetary autonomy.

In such a common market (of the type envisaged in the Commission's Report of October 1962), a country with an unfavorable geographical situation or conservative labor or businessmen would find itself in the position of Scotland today, with relatively high unemployment and probably relatively slow growth, and unable to do anything significant about the situation by the unaided efforts of its government. Such a country would either have to accept its position, or persuade its colleagues in the common market to give it special aid of one sort or another (just as Scotland tries to persuade England to do today, although by rather different political processes). Undoubtedly, in the European Economic Community, such aid would be forthcoming; but except for the very limited extent to which it is available as of right from the Social Fund, the country concerned would be at the mercy of its colleagues.

POSSIBLE METHODS WITHIN THE COMMUNITY

The logical implications of a common market system with no conceivable possibility of exchange rate changes would be that, since individual countries would not be free to determine their own national monetary and fiscal policies (except when by chance the policies they chose did not lead to excessive payments difficulties, as indeed might be the case for quite long periods of time together), then one of three things would be possible. One would be that there would be no economic planning designed to maintain full employment and to avoid inflation; to a considerable extent the "common market" of the pre-1914 world of the gold standard, free trade, and free migration was of this character. This possibility can safely be disregarded. A second possibility would be that national fiscal and monetary policies would be the outcome of bargaining between the various members of the Community; for example a member in payments difficulties might receive help (such as special loans) from the other members on condition that it did specific things, such as increasing taxes or reducing government spending. This sort of international planning has a long history, particularly in the field of co-operation between central banks, and is clearly growing in importance today, throughout the western economic system, and not merely within the European Community. The third possibility would be centrally-determined planning. Such an outcome appears to be the ultimate aim of the Commission's proposals for attaining a single unified currency and for close harmonization of fiscal measures. It is, however, perfectly conceivable that a common currency would be compatible with the second possibility just outlined (that of inter-state bargaining); for example the original intention of the United States Federal Reserve System was to create much more autonomy for the twelve member banks in regional centers than in fact has occurred. It can be argued that the high degree of centralization of policy which has in fact developed in the American monetary system has been the result of the dominance of the New York financial markets and the high degree of centralization of the political structure, so that it has not been possible in practice for individual member banks to follow substantially independent interest-rate policies, whereas in Europe there might be a common currency, together with significantly different policies in different centers.

There is, therefore, a wide range of conceivable and practicable ways of operating planning by fiscal and monetary methods in the Community (or in any other common market). Which of them is likely to develop in Europe remains highly uncertain: the only thing that seems reasonably clear is that neither of the extreme possibilities (of frequently altered exchange rates and a high degree of national autonomy on the one hand, and a United States type of centralization of monetary and fiscal policy on the other) seems at present to be the likely outcome. Frequent exchange rate changes are likely to be regarded as inconsistent with the fundamental philosophy of a common market, because they change the terms on which competition takes place between enterprises in different countries. A high degree of centralization seems equally unlikely, at least for a good many years to come, because it would either demand a much higher degree of centralization of political institutions than the individual member-states seem likely to concede, or alternatively because it would give a degree of power to a central bureaucracy which would be unacceptable to countries with democratic parliamentary institutions. Many of the most ardent European enthusiasts talk as if a political structure something like that of the United States is the inevitable outcome of the process of European integration. Undoubtedly it is a possible outcome, but the frequent assertions that it is the only satisfactory outcome appear often to conceal a poverty of imagination and a failure to realize that other outcomes are possible which would push European integration much further than the Rome Treaty itself envisages and, at the same time, take account of the fact that national interest and the sense of national identity in Europe remain so strong that no country is likely easily to accept becoming a California or a Maine.

How might such an outcome develop between the two extremes of national autonomy and frequent exchange rate changes and a United States type of centralization? Prediction is obviously impossible, but intelligent guesses can be made.

In the first place, it can be expected that exchange rate changes will be rare events, and that great efforts will be made to avoid them—but that circumstances are quite likely to arise when an exchange rate change is regarded by the members of the Community as a lesser evil than any other way open to a country in payments difficulties. For example, if one country has inflated its prices right out of line with its colleagues, as could easily happen in a couple of years of careless exuberance, or if one country has much heavier unemployment than its colleagues, then exchange rate changes might well seem the best way out. Secondly, it is reasonable to expect that the effective powers of the Commission and of the Monetary Committee on fiscal and monetary questions will become greater than the (very limited) formal powers in the Rome Treaty. One does not have to accept all the brave claims being made for additional powers, but one must accept that the Commission is in a strong enough position to obtain substantially greater powers in these fields than it now has. Thirdly, national decisions on fiscal and monetary matters will to a greatly increased extent be the outcome of bargains and negotiations between the various member governments. Planning by confrontation between national governments will become increasingly important and so will come more and more to determine the ways in which they themselves plan their domestic economies.

It is not hard to indicate in broad terms, the kind of way in which these developments might come to pass. For example, we can take the case of a country which, for some reason, finds itself in balance of payments difficulties by having an intolerably high level of unemployment. Its colleagues in the Community might help it by giving it temporary loans, perhaps through some European Monetary Fund, or perhaps by being willing to hold larger amounts of its currency than they would normally wish to do. And they might, in return for any substantial amount of aid, make the bargain that the country in difficulties shall carry out appropriate policies—such as tax changes designed to speed up economic growth or following a monetary policy which does not embarrass other countries in the Community.

With luck, it might well turn out that the difficulties would correct themselves in time—seemingly "permanent" economic prob-

lems have a habit of suddenly evaporating. But one cannot rely on
luck or self-correction. What then happens if the country's difficulties persist? Several things seem likely. One is that, as the total
amount of aid given to the country mounts, the other partners in
the Community will put in increasingly strong demands for corrective measures. The role of the Commission in formulating these
demands is likely to be powerful, and the pressure for appropriate
policies is likely to grow as it becomes more and more apparent that
the difficulties are chronic. At the same time, the country in difficulties will find it increasingly hard to resist the demands of its
colleagues and of the Commission, because it finds itself increasingly
in debt to them, so that they could force it into hopelessly awkward
difficulties if they demanded repayment of their claims.

This means that a country in really persistent difficulties would
find it extremely hard to carry out policies which ran counter to
the wishes of its colleagues—e.g. by bringing about a devaluation
which they regarded as unjustified. At the same time, the difficulties
might in time be so persistent and the accumulated credits so large,
that devaluation was the right remedy—just as today, in the common market of the United Kingdom, Great Britain would not find
it hard to accept the devaluation of Northern Ireland's pound in
order to help solve Ulster's unemployment, if only we had the
mechanisms by which such a devaluation could be brought about.
In the developed form of the European Community, as envisaged
here, devaluation would be a final remedy, which would be determined internationally and which no country could introduce arbi-
trarily, because it would be so much in debt to its colleagues by the
time devaluation came to be seriously considered, that it could not
act unilaterally without risking sharp retaliation from its colleagues,
who would be able to demand prompt repayment of its debt.

This sort of integration of policies would lie somewhere between
the extreme possibilities indicated earlier; it would not be as cen-
tralized as some people would like and, at the same time, it would
considerably reduce national autonomy in fiscal and monetary policy
and imply a much greater degree of co-ordination of national policies than we have yet known.

ECONOMIC INTEGRATION AND
THE AMERICAN EXAMPLE

Sidney Dell

Sidney Dell is at present an Assistant Director in the United Nations Department of Economic and Social Affairs. He was formerly with the United Kingdom Board of Trade and Scholar of the Queen's College, Oxford. Mr. Dell *recognizes that those who argue that economic integration will have beneficial economic effects often point to the economic success of the United States to prove their point. He investigates the three specific attributes of a large country that are supposed to bring economic progress and compares the experience of the United States and Europe. He concludes that it is not possible to attribute the high level of American productivity to the size of the American market, nor does he believe that the American experience suggests that competition will be increased or the disparities in regional per capita income reduced by economic integration in Europe. This article has been shortened with the consent of the author and certain statistical tables and other supporting material have been omitted.*

It would be wrong to suppose that the current boom in customs unions and free trade areas in several parts of the world owes all its vigor to economic theory. Much of the enthusiasm is based ultimately on political considerations. Still, in so far as economic reasoning has played its part, there can be little doubt that the spectacular success of the United States is uppermost in people's minds. It is freely asserted that American experience clearly demonstrates the advantages of a large integrated economy in exploiting to the full the benefits of mass production and specialization.

"Economic Integration and the American Example" by Sidney Dell from the *Economic Journal* (March 1959). Reprinted by permission of the author and the Royal Economic Society. The views expressed in this article are those of the author and do not necessarily represent the views of the United Nations Secretariat, to which he belongs. He wishes to acknowledge statistical help received from Mr. A. Khan and Mr. K. Moksnes.

The economic case for the integration of western Europe has been summarized as follows:

> In many fields there is an urgent need to transcend the many small national markets which are no longer adequate to cope with modern technological developments. On the other hand, many considerations, primarily political, render it impossible to lead this argument to its logical conclusion, i.e. world-wide integration. In fact, under contemporary conditions of State interventionism, economic integration can only become a reality between such like-minded nations as are already closely linked together, *inter alia*, by their economic interests. Western Europe provides such a setting, or at least an approximation to it.[1]

It has also been argued that there are certain instances, such as oil refineries and continuous wide-strip steel mills, "in which the full-time operation of a single modern plant of optimum size produces an output that exceeds the entire national demand of some of the smaller Western European countries."[2]

Notwithstanding the views of these and other authorities, the idea that the fullest exploitation of modern technology is obstructed by small national markets is not at all well-documented. It would seem in fact that even the smaller western European countries have a national demand large enough to permit optimum production of the great bulk of goods and services.[*] Such countries may satisfy their demand for goods which they cannot produce economically for themselves—whether because of inadequate size of the national market or for any other reason—through foreign trade. Nor is it out of the question for these countries to set up even such plants as oil refineries provided they can sell part of their output abroad. An excellent case in point is the Netherlands, which in 1957 produced 14.1 million tons of petroleum products, while total domestic consumption amounted to only 5.5 million tons. Such possibilities are evidently not precluded even where there are considerable tariff and quota restrictions between countries, as there are in Western Europe at the present time. A demonstration of the case for economic integration or free trade therefore requires much more than an exposition of the arithmetic of indivisible productive techniques.

---

[*] Inadequacy of national markets is, however, much more likely to be an obstacle to efficient production in certain parts of the under-developed world, such as, for example, Central America.

Some doubt was thrown by Rostas on the importance of the size of the market in explaining the pre-war United States lead in output per man-hour over the United Kingdom. He concluded that:

> There is some inter-relationship between size of the market and pro-ductivity in the sense that the greatest relative advantage in productivity in the U.S. is shown in industries where the U.S. market is relatively very big. . . . But otherwise there does not appear to be a close inter-relationship. In cases where the U.S. market is big . . . relative pro-ductivity is not above average. . . . While it is obvious from this com-parison that in certain industries the size of the market has an influence on output per worker, this is not as great as is usually assumed. If we compare the relative productivity and the size of the market in U.K. in-dustry in relation to Sweden and Holland . . . we can see that relative productivity is in no way related to the size of the market. This points to the fact that the optimum plant (or firm) and specialization can be achieved within the limits of a smaller market (output).[3]

Particularly damaging to the view that large markets generate high productivity is the fact, noted by Rothbarth[4] and others, that United States industry was more efficient than British industry as long ago as 1870, if not earlier, when the size of the United States market for manufactures was probably smaller than that of the United Kingdom. The belief that American productivity was su-perior to British productivity during the second half of the nine-teenth century receives support both from qualitative evidence based on the findings of contemporary observers[5] and from extrap-olations into past periods on the basis of the Rostas-Frankel esti-mates of current productivity relationships, combined with available data on past trends in industrial output and employment in the two countries.[6]

If it were true that under present conditions small countries are precluded from taking full advantage of the economies to be realized from mass production and specialization, this ought to be reflected in their *per capita* incomes. For example, countries ranked in de-scending order of market size ought presumably to show declining per capita incomes in terms of dollars. This is not, in fact, the case. It hardly seems necessary to go through the motions of calculating correlation coefficients to prove the point that in a world in which India, a country of nearly 400 million people, has one of the lowest per capita incomes and in which New Zealand, with a population of little more than 2 millions has one of the highest, the size of the national market bears little or no relation to productivity per head.

A second principal contention derived from American experience is that economic integration is likely to promote a higher level of efficiency by encouraging competition. Scitovsky has argued, for example, that the western European economies are less competitive than the American, that less effort is made by producers in western Europe to expand at the expense of their competitors, that the small family firm in western Europe has a staying power that makes it outlast its period of profitability, and that—

optimal plant is not likely to be built in an oligopolistic situation when the industry operates with a price structure that allows each member an adequate profit, even though productive methods are sub-optimal and costs higher than they need be. . . . In Western Europe, where national markets are often small and relations among competitors friendly and personal, there are many industries in which the above situation holds.[7]

Scitovsky concedes that quantitative evidence for this view cannot be produced. He refers to Rosenbluth's findings that the general level of industrial concentration is higher in the United Kingdom than in the United States, in the sense that industry by industry, the three largest firms account for a higher proportion of employment, on the average, in the United Kingdom than in the United States.[8] However, closer scrutiny of Rosenbluth's data suggests that the difference between the two countries is hardly of major proportions. Of fifty-seven industries examined by Rosenbluth, thirty-three had higher concentration ratios in the United Kingdom than in the United States in 1935, and twenty-four had higher ratios in the United States.

More significant, however, is the fact that the data do not seem to warrant the inference that where concentration is high in the United Kingdom, productivity is relatively low. A comparison of Rosenbluth's data on concentration with Rostas' and Frankel's results concerning relative productivity in the two countries yields no such conclusion for the few industries in which this can be done. Rosenbluth has also found that the concentration of industry is higher in Canada than in the United States,[9] and it would presumably not be

argued that the Canadian economy is subject to the same deficiencies in the field of competition as the European. Rosenbluth himself
explains the higher Canadian concentration by saying that:

> Canadian industries have fewer firms because, while the average size
> of their firms is about the same as in the United States, the industries
> themselves are much smaller. This smaller industry size, finally, reflects
> the smaller size of the Canadian economy combined with an industrial
> pattern very similar to that of the United States.[10]

It is not at all unlikely that similar considerations apply to the
United Kingdom, especially bearing in mind Sargant Florence's finding that measured in terms of the number of workers, the sizes of
firms do not differ greatly between the United States and the United
Kingdom.[11]

There are therefore no grounds for distinguishing between the
United States and western Europe in terms of the extent of industrial
concentration. If businessmen have less dynamism in western
Europe than in the United States, this has little or nothing to do
with differences in the degree of oligopoly.

It is also important not to lose sight of the fact that however well-
entrenched western European producers may be in their domestic
markets, a much larger proportion of their output than of the output
of their opposite numbers in the United States has to compete in
world markets, where it is probably far more difficult to come to
restrictive agreements than it is at home. It is not unlikely, in fact,
that competition in overseas markets by European producers, both
with one another and with United States producers, is even more
vigorous than internal competition within the borders of the United
States. In view of the importance of overseas sales in the profits of
European companies, it cannot be taken for granted that competition is a less important influence on them than it is on American
companies.

But let us even suppose it were true that imperfect markets and
restrictive business practices are more common in western Europe
than in the United States. Why should it be supposed that economic
integration would, in itself, undermine such conditions? The European Coal and Steel Community has many achievements to its credit,
but it is nowhere argued that it has led to greater competition be-

tween coal and steel producers. Nor does the adoption of the basing-point system of pricing for steel within the Community imply a particularly competitive situation. Despite the establishment of the Community, Italian steel prices seem to have been maintained at levels well above those corresponding to delivered costs from producing centers elsewhere in the Community.

One reason to expect more aggressive competition in a larger unified market is doubtless that the difficulty of arriving at and enforcing restrictive agreements among producers multiplies rapidly as the number of producers increases. There is obviously something in this argument, but how important it is in practice is not easy to tell. In the first place, some of the major industries—those, in fact, which have exhibited the greatest dynamism both in the United States and elsewhere—are precisely those in which the bulk of the output is produced by a handful of companies, and which would therefore have relatively little difficulty in coming to market-sharing and other agreements if they chose. The operations of the Brussels steel cartel are suggestive of what might be feasible in this sphere. It is not at all impossible, in fact, that some industries which are now prepared to compete vigorously on the international market so long as the solid core of home sales is assured, might feel themselves compelled to come to agreements with their counterparts abroad if they felt that foreign competition might endanger them even at home. A case in point might well be the motor-vehicle industry. This is the western European industry perhaps most frequently cited as needing the stimulus of larger integrated markets to promote efficiency through greater competition and standardization. Yet surely here is an industry which would have much less difficulty than most in maintaining restrictive agreements—even if the integrated market covered the whole of western Europe. For the number of producers is relatively small and confined to a few countries. Similar considerations probably apply in many of the other European industries.

Any argument for economic integration based upon the hypothesis that there is a more vigorous spirit of competition in the United States than in western Europe cannot therefore content itself with demonstrating that the hypothesis itself is true, but must go on to show that the difference is due to the number of frontiers in western

Europe, and not to other factors° which economic integration *per se* might do little or nothing to eliminate.

A third argument for economic integration is that it provides the most efficient means of spreading higher levels of productivity and *per capita* income throughout the territory encompassed, and that this likewise is one of the important lessons to be learned from American economic history. Uri writes that "Recent American history makes decentralization appear as the highest form of development." [12]

Before studying the American example more closely, it ought perhaps to be observed that history records plenty of examples of the opposite tendency—namely of economic polarization as the rich areas in a community or country grow continuously richer and the poor areas poorer. It has been shown, for example, that in France and Italy the gap in economic development between regions has been steadily growing while employment in industry has been expanding fastest in the most highly industrialized areas. And while regional differences in incomes and in the degree of industrialization seem at the present time to be relatively small in Germany and the United Kingdom, it is pointed out that historically, the economic development of both these countries was accompanied by economic backwardness or stagnation in certain regions, notably the area that is now the Irish Republic and the German territories incorporated in Poland and the Soviet Union at the end of World War II.[13]

Nor does a careful examination of the history of the United States suggest that the forces of economic integration in that country have been as strong as is often contended. In the first place qualitative information suggests that throughout the greater part of the nineteenth century the Southern states lagged considerably behind the rest of the country in respect to the growth of output and income. Such manufacturing as existed in the South at the end of the eighteenth century disappeared quite rapidly with the development of the plantation economy. Meantime manufacturing was expanding

---

° Many possibilities suggest themselves. It is, for example, not surprising to find in the United States the natural vitality of a population based largely upon immigrant stock, active and resourceful enough to leave their home countries and determined to succeed in a new environment.

rapidly in the North under the protection of high tariff barriers. By 1850-60 the proportion of the population engaged in manufacturing was about 1 to 8 in New England as against only 1 to 82 in the South.[14]

Investigation of data on the relative growth of urban population suggests that from about 1820 to 1880 the economy of the South was probably lagging behind the rest of the country in much the same way as has occurred in France and Italy in more recent years.

From about 1900 onward, however, the data suggest a change in the situation. This is confirmed by information on regional per capita income as a percentage of the national level available for various years going back to 1880, as shown in Table 1. No relative

Table 1

Regional per capita income as percentage of national level, 1880-1950

Area*	1880	1900	1920	1930	1940	1950
United States	100	100	100	100	100	100
New England	141	134	124	129	121	109
Middle Atlantic	141	139	134	140	124	116
East North Central	102	106	108	111	112	112
West North Central	90	97	87	82	84	94
South Atlantic	45	45	59	56	69	74
East South Central	51	49	52	48	55	62
West South Central	60	61	72	61	70	80
Mountain	168	139	100	83	92	96
Pacific	204	163	135	130	138	121
Arithmetic mean deviation of regional per capita income from national level, percentage points	45.6	36.6	25.7	31.1	25.0	16.9

* The regional definitions of the United States Bureau of the Census are used, except that the District of Columbia is omitted and Delaware and Maryland are included in the Middle Atlantic rather than the South Atlantic region.

Source: Richard A. Easterlin, "Interregional Differences in Per Capita Income, Population, and Total Income, United States, 1840-1950," in Conference on Research in Income and Wealth, *Studies in Income and Wealth*, Volume 24 (New York: National Bureau of Economic Research forthcoming), Table D-2. The entries for 1920, 1930, 1940, and 1950 are cycle averages for respectively 1919-21, 1927-32, 1937-44 and 1948-53.

improvement in per capita income in the Southern states (those referred to as the South Atlantic, East South Central, and West South Central states) is shown from 1880 to 1900. Indeed, the East South Central states did not move significantly upward, relative to the rest of the country, until the decade 1940-50. The South Atlantic states did, however, show a marked upward trend in per capita income relative to the country as a whole after 1900, and the East South Central states exhibited a weaker shift in the same direction, interrupted more sharply by the depression in agricultural prices in 1930.

There appear to be two main reasons for the relative increase in per capita incomes in the South since 1900. In the first place there were significant declines in the importance of agriculture, with its characteristically low incomes, and corresponding advances in higher paid forms of economic activity, such as manufacturing.

The second main reason lies in the substantial migration which has been taking place for well over a century from low-income to high-income areas of the United States. This has involved not only heavy population movements from rural areas to the towns but also from one region to another. The South in particular has been an enormous reservoir of man-power for other parts of the country— North and West.

Several writers have suggested that there has been a long-term tendency for per capita incomes to rise most in the areas losing population by migration, and to advance least in areas of greatest increase in population.[15] Thus Easterlin has shown[16] that during each of three periods (1880-1900, 1900-20, and 1920-50) the two lowest income areas were regions of substantial net out-migration,[17] and two other regions of relatively low income were areas of net out-migration in at least one or two of the three periods. Conversely, all the high-income regions were areas of net in-migration. Moreover, there was a tendency for the magnitudes of the migration rates to be associated with the relative income levels. Easterlin concludes that the flow of persons among regions was a persistent force making for convergence of regional income levels.

Significant though these influences were, they operated with much less force than might have been expected on the basis of the classical theory of international and inter-regional trade. Even by 1954, at the end of some eighty years of Southern industrial development, the South's share of 20 per cent in total manufacturing employment in the United States compares with a share in total population of nearly 31 per cent; and average incomes in the poorest states are still less than one-half of those in the richest.

Moreover, it seems that despite all the advantages of the unified United States market, with its free flow of labor and capital, the process of economic decentralization has been rather slow. Garver, Boddy, and Nixon found that the "index of concentration" of industry, by states, declined only moderately from 1899 to 1929.* They concluded that although there was a remarkable increase in the number of wage-earners on the Pacific coast from 1899 to 1929, there was no general decentralization of industry. The main Pacific industries were the "ubiquitous" ones—namely the industries typically dependent on local or regional markets—together with certain simple manufacturing industries based on indigenous raw materials (notably lumber). Likewise, in so far as there was an industrial drift to the South it was based mainly on textiles.

As a result of this, the South still has an industrial structure that is startlingly reminiscent of an under-developed country (though of course the average level of its per capita income is far higher than in any under-developed country). Like many of the under-developed countries, the South is most highly specialized in the textile industry, followed closely by industries processing local raw materials, especially lumber, tobacco, and petroleum; furthermore, development has been largely in the early stages of processing. The South has far less than its fair share of industries producing finished goods, especially metal products, machinery, and transport equipment—even if the term "fair share" is restricted to mean the same

* The index of concentration declined from 73.9 in 1899 to 67.8 in 1929, the limits of the index being from 50 to 100. This index is the percentage ratio of the population living outside the States (ranked in order of the density of the industrial population) in which 50% of all industrial employees are found, to the total population of the United States. Thus the lowest index of concentration— 50 implies that 50% of all industrial employees are found in states containing 50% of the total population of the United States; while the highest concentration theoretically obtainable is given by an index of 100, which implies that 50% of all industrial employees work in an area with zero population. Frederic B. Garver, Francis M. Boddy and Alvar J. Nixon, *The Location of Manufactures in the United States 1899-1929* (University of Minnesota Press, 1933).

share as of manufacturing as a whole. The special structure of production characteristic of the South is further reflected in the following data on the distribution of employment in manufacturing in 1947:

Table 2

Employment in selected industries as per cent of total employment in manufacturing

Industry group	Southern states*	United States
Textile, lumber, and tobacco products	48.1	15.5
Primary and fabricated metal products, machinery, transportation equipment, and instruments	13.3	41.0

* Alabama, Arkansas, Florida, Georgia, Louisiana, Mississippi, North Carolina, Oklahoma, South Carolina, Tennessee, Texas.

Source: Based on a special tabulation prepared by the United States Bureau of the Census for the Bureau of Business Research, University of Alabama, as cited in H. H. Chapman and associates, *The Iron and Steel Industries of the South* (University of Alabama Press, 1953).

It therefore seems to be an over-simplification to suggest, as Uri does, that United States experience reveals decentralization as the highest form of economic development. It is at least conceivable that had the South been able to limit imports of capital goods from the North, the low-income agricultural economy of the South would have yielded to industrial development much more than it in fact has, the industrial structure of the South would today be much less unbalanced, and the South would have, under its own control, more of the industrial and other facilities essential to promote cumulative growth and a more rapid narrowing of the per capita income gap between South and North. What is surely remarkable about the gap is not that it was reduced from 1880 to 1950, but that it has lasted so long in the face of the competitive forces prevailing in the most dynamic economy in the Western World.

The above discussion relates to the long-term trend toward converging per capita incomes in the United States from 1880 to 1950. There is, however, strong reason to doubt whether this particular trend can be automatically projected into the future—still less used as an example to illustrate the probable consequences of economic integration in other countries. Reference to Table 1 will show that there was no reduction of regional per capita income differentials in the United States from 1920 to 1940. Since World War II, likewise, there has been little further narrowing of such differentials despite the rapid growth of the United States economy. One factor helping to offset whatever tendencies to further convergence there may have been in recent years was the decline in prices received by farmers for crops produced in terms of prices paid by them for goods and services used—from 115 in 1947 to 84 in 1955 (1910-14 = 100).

This, however, is only a contributing factor in explaining postwar developments, since private non-farm income differentials have not narrowed very much either. The main reason for this follows from what was said above regarding the industrial structure of the South. The industries of principal importance in the South are those which, on the whole, have shown much smaller rates of expansion in the postwar period than the metal-using industries found mainly in the high-income areas. Increases in factory pay-rolls in the South-east from 1948 to 1955 surpassed the country-wide average in seventeen of the twenty-one principal manufacturing industries, and matched it in two others. Yet total factory payrolls in manufacturing as a whole increased only a little more than the average for the whole country between these years, because of the unfavorable industrial structure. Similar considerations appear to hold outside the manufacturing sector; they may also help to account for the stability in regional income differentials from 1920 to 1940.

In conclusion, it seems doubtful whether regional per capita income differences are now any smaller in the United States, with its vast integrated economy, than in western Europe, with its patchwork of independent states. The data in Table 3 are suggestive in this respect. They show the dispersion of per capita personal incomes among the eight major regions into which the United States is divided by the Department of Commerce for the purposes of its regional income estimates. This is compared with the dispersion of per capita gross national product among eight of the major European countries as calculated on the basis of purchasing-power parities by Milton Gilbert and associates. The meaning of this comparison should obviously not be pushed too far. It is nevertheless striking that the coefficient of variation of per capita personal income or gross product was of a similar general order of magnitude in the two areas; and that excluding Italy the coefficient was markedly

Table 3

Variation in income and product in the United States and Western Europe in 1955

United States:	
Coefficient of variation of per capita personal income, in current dollars, among eight regions*	19.0
Western Europe:	
Coefficient of variation of per capita gross national product in current dollars, among eight countries,† based on purchasing-power parities:	
At United States relative price weights—	
All eight countries	19.1
Excluding Italy	6.0
At European relative price weights—	
All eight countries	23.4
Excluding Italy	7.3

* New England, Mideast, Great Lakes, Plains, Southeast, Southwest, Rocky Mountain, Far West, as defined in *Personal Income by States since 1929.*

† Belgium, Denmark, France, West Germany, Italy, Netherlands, Norway, United Kingdom.

Source: United States Department of Commerce, *Personal Income by States since 1929;* Milton Gilbert and associates, *Comparative National Products and Price Levels,* Table 2; OEEC, *General Statistical Bulletin,* January 1958.

lower in western Europe. Extrapolation of the data suggests that immediately before World War II regional per capita income differentials were actually greater in the United States than among the European countries listed, whether including or excluding Italy. Thus a unified market has apparently not induced any greater uniformity in the American economy than prevails in western Europe. This surprising result should in itself give pause to those who believe that the forces set up by economic integration are necessarily all-pervasive in their impact.

It does not follow from the foregoing discussion that arguments for economic integration are necessarily without merit, although a much heavier burden of proof lies upon the supporters of such arguments than has been assumed by them hitherto. What follows is that whatever benefits economic integration may bring under favorable conditions are neither as automatic nor as prompt as they are often held to be, if American experience is our guide; and that the American example cannot be held to rule out the danger of economic polarization in an integrated Western Europe.

NOTES

1. Research Directorate of the Secretariat-General of the Council of Europe. *The Present State of Economic Integration in Western Europe* (Strasbourg, July 1955), p. 94.
2. T. de Scitovsky, "Economics of Scale, Competition and European Integration," *American Economic Review*, March 1956.
3. L. Rostas, *Comparative Productivity in British and American Industry* (Cambridge University Press, 1948), p. 59.
4. Erwin Rothbarth, "Causes of the Superior Efficiency of U.S.A. Industry as compared with British Industry," ECONOMIC JOURNAL, September 1946.
5. Thus Rostas, *op. cit.*, p. 61, cites evidence that as long ago as the 1850's British observers were impressed by the unusually widespread and rapid application of machinery and mass production methods in the United States.
6. Frankel estimates that United States labor productivity probably began to forge ahead of United Kingdom productivity somewhere between 1830 and 1860. The trend he establishes in the ratio of United States to United Kingdom productivity from this period to 1955 appears to be consistent with the data given by F. W. Taussig in "Labour Costs in the United States Compared with Costs Elsewhere," *Quarterly Journal of Economics*, November 1924; Taussig shows ratios of United States to United Kingdom physical output per worker ranging from 1.2 to 2.9 for several industries in 1907-9. Marvin Frankel, *British American Manufacturing Productivity* (University of Illinois, 1957).
7. T. de Scitovsky, *op. cit.*, p. 83.
8. Gideon Rosenbluth, "Measures of Concentration," in *Business Concentration and Price Policy* (Princeton: National Bureau of Economic Research, 1955).
9. Gideon Rosenbluth, *Concentration in Canadian Manufacturing Industries* (Princeton, 1957).
10. *Ibid.*, p. 20.
11. P.Sargant Florence, *The Logic of British and American Industry*, p. 36.
12. Pierre Uri, "Harmonisation des politiques," *Revue Economique*, March 1958. Editor's translation.

13. Economic Commission for Europe, *Economic Survey of Europe in 1954* (Geneva, 1955), pp. 142, 144.
14. See Victor S. Clark, *History of Manufactures in the United States,* 1929 edition, Vol. I, p. 580.
15. See, for example, Harvey S. Perloff, "Problems of Assessing Regional Economic Progress," in National Bureau of Economic Research, *Studies in Income and Wealth,* Volume 23, p. 49. It has also been suggested by Edward F. Denison *op. cit.,* p. 178, that the absence of a trend in the dispersion of *per capita* incomes during the postwar period (discussed further below) implies that the continuation in this period of differential regional trends in total income is associated with similar population trends.
16. Richard A. Easterlin, "Long Term Regional Income Changes: Some Suggested Factors," in *Papers and Proceedings of the Regional Science Association,* Volume IV.
17. Easterlin includes both internal and international migration within the scope of his concept of net migration.

EUROPE'S PROGRESS: DUE
TO COMMON MARKET?

Alexander Lamfalussy

Alexander Lamfalussy is Economic Advisor to the Banque de Bruxelles. During the academic year 1961-62, he was Visiting Lecturer in Economics at Yale University. In this article, Mr. Lamfalussy addresses himself to the question of whether the progress made by the member countries since 1958 can be attributed to the fact that they have joined the Common Market. That they have made progress is beyond dispute. The EEC as a group has outperformed the EFTA group and the United States in such things as growth in national income, increase in industrial production, and increase in exports. However, not all members of the EEC have had economic miracles, nor does the lack of membership prevent a country from having an outstanding growth record. By comparing individual country performances before and after the Common Market began, Lamfalussy suggests that little difference in behavior can be noted. He even offers the reverse line of reasoning and suggests that the EEC has been successful because it was made up of previously dynamic countries.

It has now become quite fashionable to argue that the establishment of the European Economic Community (EEC) has *already* had a stimulating effect on the rate of growth of the six member countries, and that the widening gap between the economic performance of the Six and that of the United Kingdom may have something to do with the fact that the latter has as yet remained outside the EEC. The purpose of this article is to discuss the validity of the statistical evidence which may be put forward in support of, or against, this argument.

To sum up the conclusion in advance, my own impression is that the weight of the evidence goes against the argument. There seem to be no obvious figures which would point to a causal relationship between the establishment of the Common Market and the rapid

"Europe's Progress: Due to Common Market?" by Alexander Lamfalussy from the *Lloyds Bank Review* (October 1961). Reprinted by permission of the author and Lloyds Bank Review.

growth of its members. It seems, in fact, quite possible to argue the other way around and to suggest that it is the "inherently" high rate of growth of Continental Europe which stimulated trade between members of the EEC and made it possible to set up the Common Market, not *vice versa*.

We should, of course, bear in mind the rules of this kind of statistical game and resist the temptation to draw too many conclusions. First, we have to rely here on very general statistics; it is quite possible that the study of individual products or markets would reveal a different story. Second, one can never *prove* anything with statistics, for the reason that we cannot actually observe alternative courses of events. In this instance it means that we can only make assumptions about what would have happened *without* the Common Market, while it is possible to observe what has actually happened since the EEC treaty was signed. Last, but not least, my concern here is exclusively with statistical evidence; and there can be a lot of important events which have not yet received confirmation in the growing flow of statistical material published by various European agencies.

This latter restriction creates an awkward problem: for one knows from firsthand experience that important changes are occurring in EEC industries (in the form of joint ventures, agreements on product specialization, and so on), all of which tend to bring the actual size of production units nearer to the optimum and to speed up technological progress; yet one is unable to produce any figures which would as yet portray the effects of such developments. The result—as is usual in conflicts of this kind—is a good deal of scepticism, which may be considered healthy by some and deplorable by others.

These are important limitations to bear in mind when it comes to drawing conclusions; but the record since the signing of the Rome Treaty is well worth examination and raises many interesting questions.

PRODUCTION AND FOREIGN TRADE SINCE 1958

Let us begin by outlining, as fairly as possible, what seems to be the commonest argument put forward by those who believe that the EEC has already had a marked impact on the pace of economic growth. The statistical background is summed up in Table 1.

Between 1958 * and the first three months of 1961 industrial growth has undoubtedly been much faster in the EEC than in the

Table 1

Industrial growth and foreign trade: 1958-61

(1958 = 100)

Item	1959	1960	1961*
Indices of industrial production:			
EEC	106	119	126
EFTA	107	113	115
United Kingdom	107	114	114
Merchandise exports:†			
EEC: Total exports	111	130	139
Intra EEC trade	119	147	163
EFTA: Total exports	105	113	120
Intra EFTA trade	107	123	128
UK: Total exports	103	110	115
Exports to EFTA	108	120	129

* First quarter, seasonally adjusted, except for intra-area trade.

† At current prices.

EFTA as a whole or in the United Kingdom taken individually. The gap appeared in 1960, and widened further in 1961. Total exports by the Six have also been growing much faster than those by the Seven. Between 1958 and the first quarter of 1961 the increase was 39 per cent for the EEC, 20 per cent for the EFTA and only 15 per cent for the United Kingdom. Now, exports can safely be regarded in the case of all European countries as the decisive factor in encouraging expansion. For one thing, a satisfactory rise in export receipts improves the external balance of the country and enables the government to let home demand expand freely. On the other hand, exports usually represent a sizeable share of total demand

* The first tariff cuts and quota increases within the Common Market took place on January 1st, 1959.

and therefore exert a direct influence on home investment and on the level of activity of home industry.

It is through this second channel that the spectacular increase in trade within the EEC—63 per cent between 1958 and the first quarter of 1961—may have played an important part in stimulating over-all expansion. For the Six, trade within the area amounts to about one-third of total exports; and this third has been growing since 1958 at a yearly rate of almost 20 per cent. On the other hand, trade between the members of the Seven represents no more than one-sixth of their total exports; and even this small part grew at a yearly rate of less than 10 per cent. The "pull" effect of "intra-area" trade has thus been much more powerful for the Common Market countries.

This, of course, is not the whole of the story. The more sophisticated advocates of the argument are quite prepared to face two objections which are likely to be raised, even if the statistical evidence is accepted as a valid starting point for discussion.

The first of these objections consists in pointing out that the two 10 per cent tariff cuts (on January 1st, 1959, and on July 1st, 1960) and the limited increases in import quotas could hardly have produced sizeable changes in the trade flows as early as 1959 and 1960. This is especially doubtful as (1) in some cases the tariff reductions have been offset by an increase in compensatory taxes, (2) some of the tariff cuts and quota increases have also been applied to imports coming from third countries, and (3) the reductions were calculated by reference to the tariff level of January 1st, 1957, while in the case of Germany, in particular, some tariff cuts had already taken place in the course of 1957.

The answer given to this objection is that the expansion in intra-EEC trade may have occurred as a result of advance planning. It does not seem unreasonable to assume that exporters would try to gain a foothold primarily in those markets where protective barriers are shortly to be removed. It may have seemed, for instance, more rewarding for a German motorcar manufacturer to invade the French market than to increase his sales in Britain. The reason is that it pays to get in first into a market which is to be opened gradually, even if the initial rise in sales is not profitable. This is likely to happen if the German manufacturer thinks of long-term profits and if he believes that the dismantling of trade barriers within the Common Market will proceed according to schedule. Both these views are in fact widely held.

The second objection runs on more theoretical lines. A somewhat arbitrary simplification of the main arguments of economic theory suggests that an increase in trade between the Six may have led to increased production only if one or more of the following conditions has or have been satisfied:

(*a*) There has been a growing specialization of each country in those lines of production in which it has a comparative advantage over other countries. This has led to the disappearance of inefficient producers, has enabled the efficient ones to become even more efficient by reaching an optimum size, and has therefore led to a better allocation of resources and to a rise in production per head.

(*b*) The actual or expected pressure of foreign competition has forced individual producers to rationalize and to invest, and thus to increase productivity by more than they would have done within the protected home markets. The result of this is not so much a better allocation of resources as their increase; but the final outcome is, anyway, an increase in productivity.

(*c*) If the member countries were not fully employed when the first steps were taken towards the establishment of the Common Market, the increase in capital outlay as suggested in point (*b*) may have led to an increase in effective demand and therefore to a more complete utilization of resources.

To begin with (*c*), it can be easily argued that the Six were not fully employed in 1958. True, the European "pause" did not result in any substantial increase in unemployment; but the marked decline in the rate of growth in 1957-58 undoubtedly created excess capacity in most Continental countries. It was quite obvious, by the end of 1958, that output and productivity could be raised through a more complete and intensive utilization of labor and machinery. It can also be argued that the rise in fixed capital formation in 1959 and in 1960 played the role of a powerful driving force in accelerating economic expansion. Between 1958 and 1960, the gross national product of the EEC member countries increased by $17,200 million in terms of 1954 prices. Gross domestic fixed capital formation alone rose by $5,300 millions. As a result, the share of fixed investment in the gross national product went up from 20.1 to 21.1 per cent.

It would, of course, be impossible to prove statistically whether anything of the kind suggested under headings (*a*) and (*b*) has, or has not, taken place in the Common Market countries. One may, however, draw attention to the fact that labor productivity has been rising much faster in the EEC taken as a whole than in the United Kingdom. A rough comparison of output and employment indices suggests that the productivity of labor may have risen between 1958 and the early months of 1961 by about 24 to 25 per cent in Germany, France and the Netherlands, by 21 per cent in Italy and by 16 per cent in Belgium, compared with only 10 per cent in the United Kingdom. The difference is the more striking as it appeared basically in 1960 and 1961. True, nobody would pretend that there has been a noticeable increase in the death rate of inefficient firms; but then one would hardly expect such an increase to occur in the midst of a powerful boom. The lack of an increased mortality does not rule out the possibility that there has already been a shift of output from inefficient to more efficient producers; but such a shift will become apparent only when demand becomes less excessive.

THE ARGUMENT REVERSED

My doubts about the validity of the foregoing argument arise not so much out of any *a priori* reasoning, or because of the impossibility of "proving" any of the three points mentioned above. They stem from the feeling that the starting point for the whole train of argument is badly chosen. It is obviously not sufficient to look simply at what has happened since 1958. There would be a presumption that the Common Market was an important operative cause of the expansion during that period only if this indicated a marked improvement on previous performance. And we should expect, too, that any such increased momentum would be general, if perhaps varying in degree, to all the countries participating in the Common Market. Yet in fact, if we take a longer perspective and examine the course of events since 1950, or at any rate 1953, we can find little evidence that this has been the case.

To consider first the comparison between EEC as a group and

EFTA as a group, it is apparent that the divergence of trends over the period 1958 to 1961 (as shown in Table 1) was already apparent during the preceding five years. In other words, if an economist from another planet looked exclusively at the most significant over-all statistical time series, without knowing anything about the EEC, the EFTA and the rest, he would hardly be able to detect a kink around 1958-59 which would induce him to ask questions about possible changes in the institutional framework of European trade.

Take for instance Chart A, showing the trend of gross national

Chart A

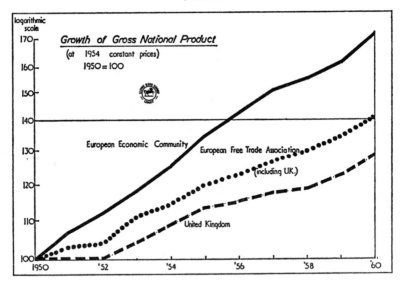

products in the EEC, the EFTA, and the United Kingdom between 1950 and 1960. It shows very clearly that the more rapid development of the Common Market countries is not the product of the last two years. In fact there has not been a single year during the 'fifties when the United Kingdom recorded a faster growth rate than the EEC. Examining the trends in greater detail, the impression given is that the reason for Britain's slower rate of progress is connected with the two periods from 1950 to 1952 and from 1955 to 1958, rather than with the most recent years. This alone suggests that anyone interested in finding out what retarded the growth of the British economy should begin by asking questions about those two critical periods.

There seems to be no recent change, either, in the pace of the EEC's development looked at independently from any comparison with other areas. It does not require the use of refined statistical tools to discover that the trend line which best fits the Common Market figures comes very near to a straight line; and since the chart is drawn on a logarithmic scale, this means a steady percentage rate of growth. True, there have been years with a higher-than-average performance: 1951, 1954, 1955, 1960. Others displayed a lower-than-average rate of growth: 1952 and 1958. On the whole, these deviations seem to fit in with traditional but very mild trade cycles; and if this assumption is adopted, the acceleration of the EEC countries' expansion in 1959-60 may be regarded as a normal cyclical upswing comparable to the one that took place in 1954-55.

Much the same impression is obtained if we look not at the record of the two groups as a whole but at the performance of individual countries. From Chart B it can be seen that between 1953 and

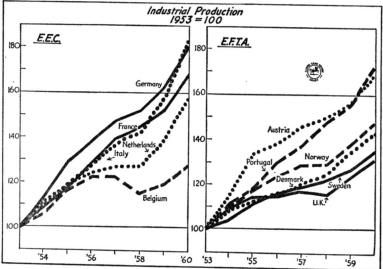

Chart B

1960 industrial production in Germany and Italy rose by 80 per cent or more; but the rate of growth was about as fast in the earlier as in the later years of the period. By contrast, industrial production in Belgium rose on balance by no more than 27 per cent—and the greater part of this increase was achieved in the years before 1956.

Within EFTA, on the other hand, Austria achieved an increase in industrial production over these years of nearly 70 per cent: not quite so spectacular an upsurge as that of Germany and Italy, but slightly greater than that of France. At the other end of the scale, the expansion in the U.K. was no more than 30 per cent. Even so, this was a little more than the Belgian increase. The pattern for the two countries is in fact remarkably similar: a reasonable rate of growth up to 1955, then some years of marking time (or in the Belgian case an actual decline), followed by renewed expansion after 1958.

The Belgian example shows that membership of the Common Market does not automatically ensure exceptionally rapid growth. On the other hand, it may well be that the Belgian record would have been even less impressive without the Common Market. Incidentally, it is worth remembering that the U.K. is by far the largest member of EFTA (accounting for about three-quarters of that group's total industrial production), whereas Belgium is one of the smaller units of EEC. Hence the similarity of their performance is bound to be reflected, statistically, in a poorer showing for EFTA taken as a group than for EEC taken as a group.

❅   ❅   ❅

Let us now turn our attention to the external trade of the two groups, as set out in Chart C, which shows the development of trade within the EEC, and of trade between the EEC and the EFTA, for the period 1953 to 1960.

It may be useful to say a few words about the reasons for selecting precisely these three sets of figures. The main reason is that, if the Common Market had already had an impact on the trade flows, one would expect to find this impact reflected mainly in a more rapid growth of trade between the members of EEC than of trade between that group and EFTA. Trade between Western European countries is composed mainly of industrial products; and although it would be a gross oversimplification to suggest that we can disregard the commodity composition of imports and exports, it seems reasonable to assume that there are numerous possibilities of substitution and hence great scope for trade diversion. There would be similar

Chart C

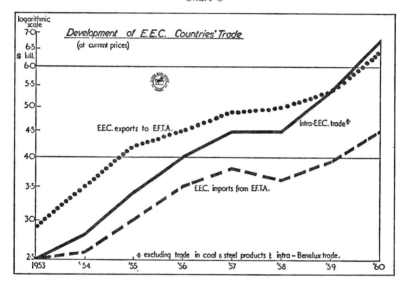

possibilities of substitution in trade between the Six and the United States. It seems wiser, however, not to attempt such a comparison, since the trade flows between Western Europe and North America were so greatly disturbed by the Suez crisis in 1956-57, and by the expansion of European automobile exports to the United States, that it is difficult to make valid generalizations about trends. Development within Western Europe, as shown in Chart C, has been more even and much less disturbed by chance occurrences.

As regards intra-EEC trade, the figures shown on Chart C exclude both intra-Benelux trade (which had become almost completely free at the beginning of the 'fifties) and trade in the products covered by the European Coal and Steel Community, which became free (with minor exceptions) in 1953. This precludes the objection that the rapid increase in intra-EEC trade *before* 1958 may have owed something to the expanding merchandise flow between Belgium and the Netherlands and to the well-known stimulating effect of the ECSC treaty, which brought about a marked growth in the exchange of steel products, especially between 1952 and 1955.

Chart C goes a long way to confirm the story told by Chart A. It shows clearly that the slower development of EEC imports from the EFTA (compared with the expansion of trade between the EEC countries themselves) did *not* begin in 1958. It had started in fact as early as 1954 and had become quite obvious in 1957-58. Between 1953 and 1958, trade between the member countries of the EEC had already increased by 80 per cent, while imports from the EFTA had risen by only 44 per cent, or about half as rapidly. It is striking to see that between 1958 and 1960 intra-EEC trade increased by 51 per cent, while imports from the EFTA rose by 25 per cent: i.e., again about half as fast.*

It is also worth considering the development of intra-EEC trade by itself. The 51 per cent growth that occurred between 1958 and 1960 is no doubt spectacular; but it so happens that there had already been another two-year period—from 1954 to 1956—which registered a 44 per cent rise, only a little less than that between 1958 and 1960. Since the period from 1954 to 1956 corresponds to the

* Looking at the same facts from a different viewpoint, the table below shows imports (excluding coal and iron products and intra-Benelux trade) drawn from other EEC countries as a proportion of total imports from EEC, EFTA and North America. For EEC as a whole, the proportion rose from 36 to 40 per cent in the five years to 1958 and further rose to 44 per cent in the succeeding two years; there were, however, striking differences in the trends for individual members:

IMPORTS FROM OTHER EEC COUNTRIES AS A PERCENTAGE OF
COMBINED IMPORTS FROM THE EEC, THE EFTA
AND NORTH AMERICA
(excluding trade in ECSC products)

IMPORTING COUNTRIES	1953	1958	1960
Germany	38%	38%	41%
France	33	42	48
Italy	31	33	42
Benelux	44	50	54
EEC total	36	40	44

upward phase of the previous trade cycle in Continental Europe, it seems as likely as not that the rapid growth of trade between the EEC countries in 1959 and 1960 was brought about by the normal cyclical upswing, rather than *vice versa*.

The plausibility of this way of thinking is enhanced if we look at the way the cyclical recovery took place in Europe as a whole. Fixed capital expenditure rose in the EEC countries from $29,900 millions in 1958 to $35,200 millions in 1960, i.e., by 18 per cent. But there was also an increase in capital outlay in other OEEC countries, from $16,800 to $19,700 millions: i.e. by a little more than 17 per cent. There is no *prima facie* evidence suggesting that the 1959-61 investment boom in Europe should be attributed to the stimulating influence of the Common Market, unless we are prepared to argue that the British, Swedish, or Austrian investment booms are the result of a reflex of self-defense. But this does not sound very plausible.

By analogy with the trade cycle argument, it would even be possible to turn completely upside down the reasoning set out in the preceding section. We could assume that, for a variety of reasons, the member countries of the Common Market have had a high "autonomous" propensity to grow. Germany, for instance, may have

Chart D

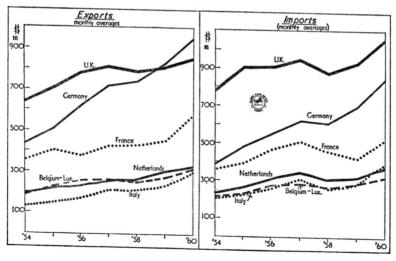

had large labor reserves, relatively low wages, and only little military expenditure to carry; Italy and the Netherlands may have grown under the pressure of a rapidly expanding population and rather low wages; and so forth. Demography, wage levels, politics, a wider scope for industrialization—all these may have acted as stimuli to rapid growth. Once this growth started, it became quite normal for the countries concerned to increase their imports from each other. And, the argument would continue, it is this "natural" tendency toward increased integration, coupled with a strong belief in further growth, that has made it possible to establish the Common Market, and to make the first tariff cuts and quota increases a more or less painless process. The *primum mobile* thus would be "autonomous" growth rather than the move toward a Common Market.

The main problem raised by this approach is to find out what the "natural" tendency toward greater integration may mean. The difficulty appears clearly in connection with the slower development of EEC imports from the EFTA countries. If growth calls for greater imports, why should the EEC countries have increased their imports from the EFTA less rapidly than from each other long before 1958? Geography might perhaps provide part of the answer, although this would hardly fit in with the fact that EEC *exports* to the EFTA have expanded more vigorously than EEC purchases from the EFTA group. Nor does it appear that the reason should be sought in the commodity composition of EFTA exports. It would rather seem that something went wrong with the competitive position of the EFTA countries as a whole, or of the United Kingdom taken individually.

Now this is, of course, a highly debatable assumption. "Competitive position" is not a very precise phrase, and if we define it more precisely (by reference, for example, to the level of labor costs per unit of output, or the level of export prices), we find it extremely difficult to measure. It seems nevertheless fairly certain that the United Kingdom's competitive position (relative to the EEC) *worsened* between 1953 and 1959, at least if we mean by this that British labor costs per unit of output or British export prices have risen more rapidly than those of the EEC as a whole.* Worsening

---

* Sir Donald MacDougall, *The Dollar Problem: A Reappraisal*, Essays in International Finance, Princeton, November 1960, pp. 17-20.

does not necessarily mean that the absolute *level* of the significant British prices became too high somewhere between 1953 and 1959; for no one really knows whether they had not been too low in 1953. The worsening has, however, been quite substantial in relation to France, Italy, and Germany, i.e. to the three main Common Market countries; so that these three countries may by 1959 have achieved a competitive advantage over Great Britain.

If this were so, the pieces of the puzzle would fall into a nice pattern. We could say that, for reasons proper to each of its member countries, the EEC achieved both a faster economic growth and an improvement in its competitive position relative to the main EFTA country, the United Kingdom. The faster growth brought about a rapid increase in imports, and these came naturally from those countries which were able to supply them more cheaply, i.e. from other member countries. The improvement of the EEC's competitive position *vis-à-vis* the United Kingdom resulted in a rapid expansion of the Common Market's exports to the EFTA, in spite of the rela-

Chart E

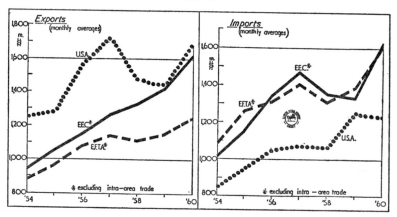

tively slow expansion of this latter area. The improvement of the EEC's balance of trade with the EFTA,† and the rapid growth of trade between the member countries, made the establishment of the Common Market attractive and an easy success.

† EEC exports to the EFTA exceeded imports by $400 millions in 1953. The surplus reached $1,400 millions in 1958 and $2,000 millions in 1960.

There can be little doubt that the favorable external position of the EEC area as a whole had been an important factor in encouraging the Six to join forces and to establish an economic union. The combined current external balance of the EEC countries has shown a surplus every single year since 1951. In periods of full (or overfull) employment, such as 1956-57 and 1960, the surplus fell below the average; but the balance has never run into the red since 1951, not even during the Suez crisis.

Table 2

External balance on current account of the EEC
(In U.S. $ [billions] at 1954 prices and 1954 exchange rates.)

Item	1950	1951	1952	1953	1954	1955	1956	1957	1958	1959	1960
Exports of goods and services	15.5	18.3	19.0	21.0	24.3	27.2	28.9	32.1	33.5	37.4	42.4
Imports of goods and services	16.0	17.0	18.2	19.9	22.7	25.3	28.7	31.3	31.7	35.0	41.2
Surplus (+) or deficit (−)	−0.5	+1.3	+0.8	+1.1	+1.6	+1.9	+0.2	+0.8	+1.8	+2.4	+1.2

The fact that there has been a steady external surplus does not, of course, by itself prove that the EEC countries as a whole have enjoyed a continuing competitive advantage over other industrial areas. Any country can have a surplus on current account, provided it is prepared to keep a sufficiently tight rein over internal demand; but for high-cost countries, or for countries with an unfavorable commodity composition of exports, an external surplus could be achieved only at the cost of some degree of unemployment. Now, the striking thing is that (except for some cyclical fluctuations) unemployment has been strongly declining within the Six. France and the Netherlands never had very much; but Germany's unemployment fell from an average of 1.4 millions in 1950-52 to 230,000 in 1960, that of Italy from 1.8 to 1.5 millions, and that of Belgium from 167,000 to 110,000. In spite of a severe labor shortage in 1960, the EEC countries proved able to earn in that year a current external surplus of $1,200 millions.* This strongly suggests that in one way or another the EEC has been enjoying a competitive advantage *vis-à-vis* the rest of the industrial world as a whole. But unemployment had already begun to decline in Germany and Belgium around 1954-55, without any corresponding deterioration in the current balances of these two countries. Once again, therefore, there is no conclusive evidence that the establishment of the Common Market had anything to do with this favorable position.

On the contrary, the case of France confirms our earlier suspicion that it is much more fruitful to think the other way around. In 1956 and 1957 France ran into a big external deficit and, although the Treaty had been ratified by the national parliaments by the end of 1957, there was a great deal of uncertainty in 1958 about the actual application of the first trade concessions scheduled for the beginning of 1959. However, France managed to close her inflationary gap in the second half of 1958 and she restored her competitive position by devaluing at the end of the same year. This enabled her to reap the benefits of the rapid increases in productivity which had taken place between 1953 and 1957, but whose beneficial effects had been masked until 1958 by the inflationary pressure. As a result, the first tariff cuts were put into effect on January 1st, 1959, without causing the slightest disturbance.

It is doubtful whether this would have been possible had the improvement of France's competitive position hurt any other member country. But the competitive position of the rest of the Community seems to have been strong enough to support the revival of French competition in all markets. The vanishing of the French deficit thus did not bring about any marked deterioration in the current balance of the other EEC countries. The impact, if any, could be exported outside the Community to other industrial areas; nothing happened to prevent the EEC countries from continuing to expand and to increase their trade with each other.

---

* At 1954 exchange rate and 1954 prices. At *current* prices and exchange rates the surplus was $3,100 millions, as against $2,600 millions only in 1958, i.e. in a year of higher unemployment.

CONCLUSIONS

So far so good. The counter-argument looks neat enough and at least as plausible as the argument we set out to criticize. I should, however, be reluctant to conclude without once again calling attention to two limitations of this analysis, already mentioned at the beginning of the article.

First, the rather negative conclusion about the effects of the Common Market to date is not confirmed by direct experience in business. Anybody who has had the opportunity of closely watching the rapidly changing mentality of Continental industrialists, or to observe the flood of joint ventures and capital expenditure which in all cases are justified with reference to the Common Market, cannot but be unhappy about the apparent air of scepticism in previous sections of the article. It would, of course, be easy to argue that the recurring references to the Common Market in company reports or public speeches do not necessarily prove that the actual decisions have really been motivated by the establishment of the EEC, and that the effect of investment decisions taken in 1959 or 1960 is in any case unlikely to become apparent in published statistics before another couple of years. Yet industrialists seem to be so convinced that something new is emerging in Continental Europe that it would be foolish to project into the future the time series analyzed in this article without bearing in mind that the EEC *may* bring about quite substantial changes in trade flows and in growth rates during the 'sixties.

This is the more relevant as one could not claim to have "proven" —even statistically—the validity of the conclusions suggested. There remains the eternal doubt raised by the *ceteris paribus* assumption, which in the present case means that we are unable to observe what would have happened *without* the establishment of the EEC. The "autonomous" stimuli to growth may have become exhausted by 1958-59, and that would have meant an actual slackening in the rate of growth but for the new stimulus provided by the opening of the Common Market.

This objection should not be dismissed light-heartedly. Even if we believe that it has not applied hitherto, it may well become of growing validity in the years ahead. Recently, important changes have taken place in some of the growth-leading Continental countries. After years of an easy labor market, Germany has entered since 1960 into a period of acute labor shortages. German labor costs have been rising since 1959 more rapidly than those of most other European countries, and there has also been a rise in German prices. There are signs that a similar development is on its way in the Netherlands and in Italy, while it becomes clear that France has for some time been losing some of the advantage secured by the devaluations in 1957-58.

If this trend continued, EEC would be likely sooner or later to lose at least part of its competitive advantage *vis-à-vis* other industrial areas. While this would be a good thing for the sake of international equilibrium, such a development would lead the EEC countries into rougher waters. If their combined external balance became less favorable, and if exports to third countries provided a weaker stimulus to expansion, we should soon begin to know whether the opening of the Common Market has, or has not, promoted the expected transfer of resources and so helped to raise productivity. So long as the present boom conditions prevail (combined with strong external surpluses), judgement must be suspended. It is the next pause or recession which will be the real testing time, both for the Common Market's success and for its internal cohesion.

INTERNATIONAL INTEGRATION
AND THE MODERN STATE

Max Beloff

Max Beloff is Gladstone Professor of Government and Public Administration in the University of Oxford. His publications include Europe and the Europeans (1957), New Dimensions in Foreign Policy (1961) *and* The United States and the Unity of Europe (1963). *Professor Beloff begins his article by recognizing the resurgence of nationalism in Europe and the crisis between the advocates of European federalism and the advocates of a confederation. He examines the meaning of these political terms—pointing out their differences. He suggests that progress can be made by not trying to make the real world fit theoretical abstraction, but by trying to work out solutions to problems as they arise without much thought to ideal systems. He suggests that appropriate instruments can be developed as they are needed.*

We are now at a very different stage in the history of international integration to that at which matters stood in the Spring of 1962. Instead of going forward to an integrated Western Europe closely linked with the United States in an Atlantic Community, we are entitled to question even the capacity of those institutions already created to survive in face of the renewed accent upon national self-sufficiency of which General de Gaulle has made himself the most prominent, though by no means the only, spokesman. It looks as though we had underestimated the extent to which even in continental Europe it was still the nation rather than any wider grouping that commanded the allegiance of the masses; and in North America there is as yet no sign that either the United States or Canada is prepared for any sacrifice of sovereignty.

But if our time-scale has altered, this does not necessarily mean that we should lose interest in these problems. For it is probable that

"International Integration and the Modern State" by Max Beloff from the *Journal of Common Market Studies* (Vol. II, No. 1). Reprinted by permission of the Journal of Common Market Studies.

the same kind of experience and pressures that brought about the creation of the EEC, NATO, and so on will eventually bring about new efforts in a similar direction. Not only in Europe and in the North Atlantic area but in other parts of the world as well, and irrespective of particular ideologies, the need for political institutions transcending the individual State has been widely felt. "Integration" is thus a general problem of modern politics, and however inappropriate the word may seem for the process it denotes, it is certainly something that the student of politics cannot simply ignore or avoid.

The first of the broad theoretical problems upon which our experience of the post-war institutions may cast some light is the question of sovereignty. I have already been forced to use the word in this paper; but I have done so in a rather precise sense. What I mean by saying that the United States would not, for all the talk of an Atlantic Community, surrender its sovereignty in order to bring it about, is that the U.S. would not be prepared so to amend its constitution as to enable decisions binding upon its government, or directly upon its citizens, to be taken by processes over which it would not retain an ultimate veto. Given a conflict between some direction by an international organization and what the Federal Government of the United States decrees, there is no doubt to which order American thinking would give priority. And therefore Americans have taken pains not to be put in a position of this kind.

In theory of course this position is one that can be adopted by any political community; we have had a recent example of a *reduction ad absurdum* of the sovereignty argument in the conflict between Monaco and France. But for practical purposes the value of maintaining the pure doctrine of state or national sovereignty must depend upon circumstances. What is plausible in the case of the United States or the Soviet Union is less plausible in the case of Canada or Poland. In other words, under modern conditions both from the point of view of the people's livelihood and from the point of view of defense, interdependence is today a much commoner experience than independence. The question is not whether this is true, but what follows from it in the sphere of government. Is it possible to ignore the fact of interdependence in the structure and working of our institutions? Some people are minded to say "yes." Their argu-

ment is at bottom an argument from situations of crisis. They take
the State or more often the Nation as the ultimate reality—like the
individual in society. Normally, they admit, the State's concerns are
interlocked with those of other States—men, goods, techniques move
freely between them. Agreements are entered into to facilitate such
movement. But just as man is born alone and dies alone, so in the
last resort the individual community must be in a position to decide
its own fate. Whatever parcels of sovereignty it has let go, it must
be able to recover. And this doctrine of the last resort will obviously
affect the type of international organization into which a State will
be prepared to enter. But it may be asked if this is a rational way
to behave. Just because man is in the last resort on his own, he is
not normally inhibited from entering into tight social relations within
a family, a tribe, or a political community of some kind. He accepts
that his normal manner of life will be a life based upon interdependence and creates his social institutions accordingly.

Now the answer that will be given here is that if one sincerely
believes in interdependence, then one ought to accept the logic of
the position and declare for all-out federalism. And there are cases
in which this argument is perfectly reasonable. No one would seriously, I suppose, advocate destroying the federal bonds between the
cantons of Switzerland or the States of the American Union. But
there are two reasons for refusing to accept the federal formula as
an all-inclusive one.

In the first place, it presupposes that the interdependence between the communities in one grouping is overwhelmingly more
important than any links which may bind them, or some of them,
to other communities outside the grouping. Perception of the truth
of this fact where Britain is concerned has been an impediment to
believing that Britain could be fitted into a European federal system.
Not, be it noted, because of "sovereignty" or "independence," but
because of the difficulty of reconciling Britain's membership of a
federation with other aspects of its condition of interdependence
—its relations with Commonwealth countries and with the United
States.

In the second place the historic development of federal systems
has enabled the legally-minded to encompass them with particular
definitions as to what they are, and are not, which may not be

what is needed when we come on to considering the institutional forms required to express other types of interdependence, notably that between nation-States with a very high level of self-consciousness, and a very keen awareness of the desirability of retaining certain elements of difference between themselves and their neighbors.

But federalism, in a broader sense, is not so much a political system as a method of political analysis.

If certain powers are allotted to a central government, acting directly upon the individual citizen, while other powers are retained by lesser units, we have, it is said, a federation. But although this idea is helpful to the lawyer in making decisions as to the legitimacy of particular acts of government, it does not necessarily tell one the most important things about a particular society. We all know that modern societies are highly complex, that power is distributed not merely on a territorial basis but also among occupational and other groupings which may be theoretically amenable to some legal sovereign, but which in fact the political authority can only deal with by a judicious combination of persuasion and coercion, with persuasion normally playing the leading role. Are President Kennedy's difficulties with the State of Mississippi really of a wholly different kind to the British Government's difficulties with the National Union of Railwaymen? And yet Britain is often regarded as the unitary state *par excellence.*

Federalism as a method of government is thus simply a systematization of one particular form of distributing the powers of decision-making within a complex modern society. It may be traced not only in the relations between the unit of a formal federation and the central authority, but also within the units themselves. The question that has to be asked is whether the arrangements made are such as conduce to efficiency in decision-making without the loss of the consent which is necessary if decisions arrived at are to be effective. If one chooses to call the European Communities federal or quasi-federal, or to say that they are aiming at political federation, this must be thought of in political, rather than in legal, terms if the impact upon the present or future members of such a grouping is to be assessed correctly.

There is indeed a double problem here of which the two strands are not always successfully disentangled. First, there is the question of the most efficient unit in relation to the subject-matter of particular decisions. Second, there is the question as to the level of government at which people are willing to allow decisions to be made which they will accept as binding. The answer need not be identical in the two cases. But efficiency itself may be impaired if the second point is ignored.

I think myself that the phrase "supra-national," which was originally used to describe the institutions of the Coal and Steel Community, despite their rather pronounced element of federalism, is likely to be of more use than the word "federal." The distinction between inter-national and supra-national must not, however, be pushed too far. What supra-national means is that there is a recognized interest within a political grouping of several nations which is different from, or distinguishable from, the interests of any one of them, and which thus claims institutional expression. The idea expressed by the word inter-national means that there are interests which the nations have in common, but which they can only arrive at through processes of discussion and voting. But in the United Nations itself, which like its predecessor the League, was thought of as international rather than supra-national, an element of supra-nationalism has undoubtedly come in with the attempt by the late Mr. Hammarskjöld to increase or develop the responsibilities of the Secretariat so as to overcome the difficulties which the ideological conflict in the world had placed upon the development of the international machinery, the Assembly and the Security Council. It was the lack of such a supra-national component in the OEEC as it ultimately developed that led in part to the decision by the Six to proceed by themselves in the economic field. And one could argue that it is the search for a supra-national element within NATO which is the crux of the present difficulties about the possession and control of the ultimate weapons of deterrence.

The governmental mechanisms of the Coal and Steel Community and subsequently of EURATOM and the Common Market owe something to federalism, particularly in the first case, as they owe something to the idea of a supra-national element. To federalism and its example they owe the fact that they are based upon written instruments subject to the interpretation of a court of law, just as is the case with the federal constitutions of the United States or Australia. But despite the fears that have been expressed on this score, it is difficult to see how the Court can become a major instrument for breaking down the defenses of the social structures of individual communities except where political decisions leading in this direction have already been taken. I think that people have in mind the example, for instance, of the U.S. Supreme Court and its role in the segregation issue. But even here, while it is true that it is ruling against the mores of a particular community—whatever we may think of these mores—it is doing so by interpreting a basic document of the whole system, namely the Federal Constitution.

The supra-national element is, of course, that represented by the High Authority of the Coal and Steel Community, or the Commissions of the Common Market and EURATOM. It rests, as did Mr. Hammarskjöld's views upon the possible role of the Secretariat of the United Nations, upon the belief that despite the historic rivalries of the modern nation-states, individual men can be drawn from them and trained to see and serve the interests of the group as a whole without regard to the particular concerns of their country of origin. I see no experience which would lead one to believe that this is an artificial concept, though it must clearly depend upon finding persons who place high in their list of values the promotion of the unity of the group. It is only, as in the case of nationals of totalitarian countries, where ideology is paramount that the interests of the country of origin will remain paramount over the interests of the entire group. That is why the task of elevating the Secretariat of the United Nations, which must contain representatives of Communist countries, is so much more difficult than the building up of a common outlook among the servants of the European communities.

The difficulty lies not in conception of policy, but in its authorization and execution. To some extent the difficulty about authorization has in the case of the Coal and Steel Community, and of the Common Market, been met in advance by the precise nature of the tasks entrusted to the organizations and by the actual timetables of accomplishment laid down for them, but even so, either keeping to the timetable or even accelerating it, has depended very largely upon the assent of the individual governments through their representation upon the three Ministerial Councils, and the relations between the Commission and the permanent delegations of the member countries or their ministerial chiefs must at all times be an intimate one. The governments cannot be excluded from policy-making when decisions in these fields demand action in so many others.

Equally, this is true of execution, since the body of the work done by the Common Market authorities relates to the actions of governments and instruments—for instance, the customs authorities of the different countries—and does not to the same extent as in the Coal and Steel Community operate upon individual firms. But it would appear from the relative smoothness with which a good deal of the programme of both has been implemented, that appropriate techniques of collaboration have not been lacking there either. Once again, one can use the federal analogy, since in modern federations the degree of overlapping responsibility between the center and the unit, and of the overlapping of actual administrative functions, is very high indeed. A recent work by an American scholar suggests, as a matter of fact, that this was true even in the nineteenth century United States, when the lawyers and political theorists were still depicting the federal and the State governmental machines as totally separate from each other.[1]

I suspect that behind the dramatic if fruitless reversal of British policy in 1961, and the decision to try to enter the Common Market, we could discover a change of mind in the higher levels of the British civil service. For this ability to operate a complex machinery of government with responsibility spread among a number of different authorities, and involving the arts of the negotiator as well as of the administrator, is certainly not alien to the Whitehall spirit. Whether a civil servant's experience has been in the complexities of Commonwealth relations, or at the more humdrum plane of working with local authorities in health or housing, this kind of thing has been a commonplace of the daily round. The intellectual challenge of doing the same thing at the international level must have been hard to resist.

The real difficulties have not been those inherent in carrying out the basic programs of the original European communities in so far as these figure in precise terms in the treaties. Where they have run into trouble has been in relation to those things which are either prescribed in very general terms such as the common agricultural policy, or the equalization of social conditions in an upward direction, or where the group has had to function as a unit in its relations with the external world or particular parts of it, and make new decisions for which the Treaties provide no clear prescription.

Fundamentally it would appear that five of the countries concerned argue that further problems of this kind can be solved by developing the same procedures of decision-making as have proved their effectiveness in relation to the original aspects of the Communities. The French Government has taken the view that while the grouping as a whole should have a common political orientation this can only be arrived at by other methods.

Here we come up against another of the words that so confuse the argument—the word "confederal." Now confederation is a concept much harder to define than federation. But what it has historically represented in essence is the idea that institutions can be provided through which individual governments, acting on behalf of their own countries, accept certain procedures for arriving at joint decisions which they are prepared to carry out afterwards through their own instrumentalities. In a Confederation the individual citizen need never know that his State forms part of one since the decisions that concern him are mediated through it.

The symbol as it were of Confederation has been the power to decide things by vote. I doubt if anyone would have called Confederation a system in which each member retained a veto on everything. The three European Communities tried to make up for the relative weakness of the federal or supra-national element by introducing a confederal one in the shape of the ministerial councils, and by providing in some instances for weighted voting. In the case of the EEC the requirements for unanimity were to be progressively modified as the process of instituting the Common Market progressed.

Now it is obvious that the agreement in advance to accept majority decisions provides less of a breach with the formal pattern of national sovereignty than does the "supra-national" approach. Britain has accepted it on many matters in the United Nations and in some lesser institutions. But if it provides a form of safeguard against the over-riding of the interests of a particular community, it is at the same time something of an obstacle to the development of common purposes.

Professor Christopher Hughes in his interesting inaugural lecture[2] has now suggested that the time has come to revise our traditional ideas about "confederal" as well as "federal" institutions. Federalism, he suggests, is "a classification of unitary government of the fully constitutional type." Since "the purpose of federalism is the maintenance of local cultures," things are so arranged that "illegality cannot happen," that is, that the rights of the State cannot be infringed, "without rending the whole fabric of law and order."

If this is the essential thing about a federation, or as Professor Hughes prefers to call it, a Confederation, what are we to make of what he calls a Confederacy, that is to say of a system where the confederal principle operates? In order to answer this question, Professor Hughes takes three classical examples: the United States, 1775-89; Switzerland, 1813-48; Germany, 1813-66.

The myth he is concerned to destroy is that a Confederacy is a special form of Treaty, and not a particular form of State. What he is able to show is that the Continental Congress, the Swiss Diet and the Germanic Diet all acted as though they were vested with legal sovereignty; that is to say they legislated on some internal matters and enforced their jurisdiction on matters which had not been handed over to them from the units of which their respective confederacies were composed. In the German case, indeed, some of the units were themselves the creation of the Confederacy which was an instrument of the four member-States that had an unquestioned political position of their own.

I am neither concerned nor equipped to deal with Professor Hughes' historical points; but if we assume that he is basically correct, some interesting conclusions follow. For what then appears is that the Confederacies, while rather primitive States in that they do not attempt to act within a very wide range, are powerful States in the sense that there are no legal or constitutional controls but only political controls over their actions. The Confederal authority is like an absolutist monarch; some of his subjects may be strong enough to resist, but if they are not he can get away with what he chooses to. "A confederacy then," according to Professor Hughes, "is an earlier, tougher kind of State" than what we call a Federation.

The most relevant feature of the organization of a confederacy is the centralization of authority: "You would not," writes Professor Hughes, "expect a confederacy to have a highly developed structure of parliaments, judiciary, and executive. It may play with such ideas, and all confederacies have played with such ideas, but in a crisis, and in the long run, the princely power is always with a council of ministers, sometimes to keep up the illusion of compact, called 'ambassadors.'"

Professor Hughes has some other interesting ideas to offer; notably on the "pathology" of confederacies; but I think the relevance to our present argument should now be clear. For it is obvious that without having studied Professor Hughes' lecture or done similar research into the arcana of Bernese history, that very eminent political scientist General de Gaulle has come to very similar conclusions. Whether one looks at the plan submitted by the French Government to the Fouchet committee on November 10, 1961, or at the most likely interpretation of the Franco-German treaty of January 22, 1963, it is clear that the idea of a permanent council of governments without formal constitutional or legal impediments to action, and able to act where necessary without the concurrence of all members of the group is at the heart of the de Gaulle vision of how Europe should be run.[3]

By Professor Hughes' criteria this is a confederacy even without any provision for action by weighted voting. According to M. Alain Peyrefitte (whom Mr. Roy Pryce accepts as a qualified exponent of the Gaullist view), the unanimity stage in the French plan was to be followed by weighted voting and ultimately by straight majorities.[4] But the important thing is that it discards both federalism in any of its interpretations, and the "supra-national" element in the existing European communities. The necessity for common policies is agreed, but not that of common instruments for carrying them out; the armed forces of the "confederacy" would be national or, as Professor Hughes would put it, "territorial." But still more important, these common policies would be reached by agreement at the top where the power of States and the authority of leaders would count for most, and not by a process of synthesis at many different levels, as in the Community idea.

It is also obvious that under this confederal principle, the element of popular control will be even more inconsiderable than in the European Communities as they now stand. For while the latter look toward the direct election of their Parliament, and so to a further infusion of the federal idea, the confederacy principle is quite compatible with taking a very modest view of the role of elected bodies both in respect of its own institutions and with regard to the units of which the proposed confederacy would be made up.

Fortunately we are not called upon to prophesy how all these conflicting views and aspirations will be reconciled, if at all. Nor need we go into the analogous issues relating to the Atlantic Alliance where the speed that may be required in making decisions provides a new complicating factor when possible institutions are discussed. The point I wish to raise is rather more general. Is there any way of meeting the claim which both the Federalists and the Gaullist advocates of confederacy make—though for different reasons—that there is no new way around the basic issue of all political societies —who obeys them? Either, it is said, you have the nation-state as your unit and merely delegate to some international instrument under severe restrictions such functions as you do not wish to run directly, or you accept the idea of merging your nation and its state-machine in some larger unity, with such protection for local interests as seems reasonable. Further, they will argue, this dilemma is now even harder to escape from than it was when the *Federalist* papers were written because of the vastly increased sphere within which the modern State functions: the more points at which the public authority touches upon daily life, the closer the interaction between public policy and economic and professional activity, the harder it is to imagine separate sources of legitimacy and power for the several instrumentalities required.

I do not minimize the force of these arguments. I have used them in my time, and yet, as I suggested at the beginning, there may be a case for believing that the difficulties arise from trying to adjust our view of the world of action to suit our concepts rather than our concepts to suit the world we perceive. In fact, we do contrive to live in subordination to a number of separate authorities and to take part in a number of different processes for making decisions without normally having to place them in an hierarchical order. From the individual conscience to the Assembly of the United Nations or the Pope speaking *ex cathedra* (or wherever you place your embodiment of the universal general will), there is a kind of continuum without which organized living would break down. Federalism, or, if you prefer a more general though now unfashionable phrase, political pluralism, is the common experience. Even the would-be monoliths —the Soviet Union for instance—agree to consider the point of view of the international communist movement, and find it all they can do to prevent other views and sentiments and desires from impinging upon the consciousness of the peoples under their control.

The great achievement of political theory in the West has been to build complex systems upon the simple tag: *quod omnes tanget ab omnibus approbetur.* [That which touches all, should be approved by all. Ed.] We should not let it go. If decisions can be taken municipally or by some non-governmental grouping—a professional organization for instance—then let them be taken there, and let the machinery be such as to see that all those who are concerned with the decision are given their say. And so too at the national level. But if meaningful decisions in economics or defense can only be taken at an international level, then the same considerations come into play. The decisions taken must embody the maximum degree of agreement obtainable; those who disagree must not be outraged either by the substance of the decision or by the procedure and so on. It becomes a matter of devising appropriate institutions not of reifying or deifying particular abstractions. And there is a good deal to be said for facing this need head-on rather than simply accepting the inevitability of abandoning in practice if not in theory the obsolete claim of the middle-sized nation-state to be the suitable unit for performing many of the essential functions of modern government. That we had gone a long way in this direction I have argued elsewhere.[5] That the process is irreversible seems undeniable. The most useful thing we can do in such a discussion is to see what kind of organization best corresponds both to communities which are today's realities—such as the nation—and to communities which are likely to be tomorrow's in the sense of commanding allegiance and respect—Europe, the Commonwealth, Atlantica—all or any of them.

Cujus regio, ejus religio [The sovereign determines the religion. Ed.] was never a very healthy principle; secularized it is worse; translated into economics, it is absurd. Let us begin from there.

NOTES

1. See Daniel J. Elazar, *The American Partnership* (Chicago, Ill.: University of Chicago Press, 1962).
2. *Confederacies: An Inaugural Lecture* by Christopher Hughes. Leicester University Press, January 1963.
3. This document is most easily accessible in Roy Pryce, *The Political Future of the European Community* (John Marshbank, 1962). Note especially Art. 6. "The Council shall deliberate on all questions which one or more member states have asked to have included on the agenda. It shall adopt unanimously the decisions necessary for achieving the aims of the Union. The absence or abstention of one or of two members shall not be an obstacle to the adoption of a decision. The decisions of the Council are binding upon member states which took part in their adoption. The member states upon which a decision is not binding on account of their absence or abstention may accept it at any time. The decision shall become binding upon them from that time."
4. See Pryce, *op. cit.*, pp. 52ff.
5. *New Dimensions in Foreign Policy*, London, 1961.

PART III

The Common Market and Non-Member Countries

AFRICAN ATTITUDES TO THE EUROPEAN ECONOMIC COMMUNITY

Ali A. Mazrui

Ali Mazrui is a Lecturer in Political Science, Makerere University College of East Africa, Kampala. He was formerly a Research Student at Nuffield College, Oxford. Most Africans from countries associated with the Common Market recognize the very great benefits they obtain from this association and heartily approve of the EEC. In this article, Professor Mazrui presents the views of Africans from non-associated countries who are critics of the EEC. He details three levels of criticism. Some Africans object to the very idea of a united Europe because it postpones the time when African countries will feel at a par with their old colonial masters and this feeling of equality is an important nationalist goal. Secondly, some Africans object to the fact that only part of Africa is associated with the EEC which works an economic hardship upon non-associated countries and stands in the way of pan-Africanism. Finally some Africans merely object to the terms of association which give very great short-run benefits to existing export industries, essentially raw materials, which may stand in the way of needed industrial development.

It is difficult to be sure of the degree of opposition that exists in Africa to the European Economic Community and what it is supposed to represent. But at least one can say that within Common-

"African Attitudes to the European Common Market" by Ali A. Mazrui from *International Affairs* (January 1963). Reprinted by permission of the author and International Affairs.

wealth Africa the EEC is suspect to Nigeria, the largest country on the West Coast; to Tanganyika, the largest on the East Coast; and to Ghana, perhaps the best educated and ideologically the most in-fluential country in Commonwealth Africa. Outside these countries there are Africans who are uncertain whether to condemn or commend the EEC. But this article is more concerned with the uncertainties of those who have already declared their opposition to the Community—whether to condemn it on these grounds or on those.

There are in fact three major levels of objection to the EEC apparent in the attitudes of its African critics. There is, first, the objection which, in its extreme form, amounts to virtually complete opposition to the idea of a united Europe. Secondly, there is the attitude which declares indifference to whether Europe unites or not, but which objects to Africans being directly linked to a united Europe. The third attitude of objection concedes an African need to be linked to the prosperity of a united Europe, but not on the terms implied by formal associate membership—at least, not as that is now understood. These three attitudes do not necessarily reflect opinions held by different Africans; they are often discernible in the arguments of the same people.

*   *   *

The attitude of objection to the very idea of a united Europe is the least expressed—one can almost say the least "conscious" part—of African criticism of the EEC. It might well be asked whether pan-Europeanism can be bad for Europe if pan-Africanism is good for Africa? Yet the relevant question in the African's mind is not whether pan-Europeanism is good for Europe but whether it is good for Africa. And this question comes right up against the basic presuppositions of African nationalistic thought. After all, nationalism generally derives its impulse from opposition to or competition with other "nations." African nationalism started with the element of opposition rather than rivalry as its motive force. But with the attainment of at least formal independence by most of Africa rivalry has been slowly displacing opposition. To the extent that there is now a Nigerian nationalism and a Ghanaian nationalism, the rivalry may be strictly inter-African—motivated by what the nationalists themselves would, in their cooler moments, condemn as instincts which are at once fratricidal and suicidal. To the extent that there is an *African* nationalism, however, the rivalry is primarily with the Western Europe that once ruled Africa.

African nationalism seeks to achieve and to maintain equality with Europe. African unity was conceived ultimately as a means for gaining that equality. Essentially it was a case of creating a united Africa to be the equal of a divided Europe. There has been, in the language of African unification, the implied assumption that even if a united Africa, materially on a level with a divided Europe, did not prove equality in technological capacities, it would at least have established African *superiority* in terms that can almost be described as "ethical." The (Nigerian) Action Group Policy Paper on a West African Union issued in 1960 could thus view the creation of such a Union as a means by which Africans were to prove to the world that "Negro states, though the last to come, are the first to use their brains for the conquest of the forces that have kept men apart." [1] Such Negro states were to have been almost the first multi-lingual sovereign states willingly to renounce their sovereignty for the unity of at least one group of peoples. To that extent they would have established superiority over a Europe which, in recent times, had had two enormously costly civil wars—a Europe which still remained in acute competition both within itself and in the advantages each little segment of Europe sought from the outside world. With some African nationalists it had even become a matter of racial vindication to achieve unity before "civilized" Europe achieved it— thus proving that Africa had a greater capacity for transcending "primitive tribalism" than the Europe that had taunted and laughed at Africa for that very "tribalism" for so long.

The Charter of Casablanca pledged its signatories "to promote the triumph of liberty all over Africa and to achieve unity." About a year before the Action Group of Nigeria was in its turn arguing that Nigeria's own sovereignty was not to be an end in itself but a means toward objectives which included winning respect for people of African descent "by the creation of a Negro world." The Action Group declared that "we must ensure that we make a distinct and worthwhile contribution to the civilization of the world." [2] For Nigerians to make such a contribution, Nigerians had to unite. But in itself Nigerian unity, as just another nation-state, could not be

distinctive. For Africans to make a contribution, Africans had to
unite.

The appearance of the EEC cuts right across this African nationalist ambition to achieve equality with the old, divided Europe. It
also deprives the Africans of the hope of achieving ethical superiority over Europe by attaining unity first and thus neutralizes this
hope as a motive force in the drive for African union. This, then,
is the frustrating significance of the EEC in relation to what was to
be the *intrinsic* value of African unity as a moral achievement.

o   o   o

But what of the significance of the emergence of a united Europe
in relation to the *instrumental* value of African unity? Here again
the Action Group, whatever its shortcomings, was not unrepresenta-
tive of African nationalistic thinking in viewing the first end of
African sovereignty as being to bridge in the shortest possible time
the *"technological"* gulf between Africa and the more developed
world.[3] If a united Europe would make the gulf between Africa and
the richer nations even greater, that fact alone could be enough to
make it humanly difficult for a proud African to welcome with enthusiasm the prospect of a united Europe. Even as matters now
stand the gap between the rich nations that are already in economic
orbit and the poor ones that have yet to take off is growing wider
rather than narrower. If the development of the Western world had
sparked off what is now widely called "a revolution of rising expectations," the more developed the Western world now becomes the
higher will rise the expectations of the poor countries as to what is
humanly possible—and the greater will be the gulf in those countries, first, between the aspirations they have and the actualities they
face, and, secondly, between themselves and the richer nations
abroad. As Mr. Nehru said at the 1962 Commonwealth Prime Ministers Conference, "anything which widens the gap between the richer
and the poorer countries is likely to lead to trouble because the
poorer and developing countries will feel it is being done at their
expense." [4]

It may indeed be unfair to expect Europe to remain technologi-
cally static to allow the poorer parts of the world to catch up with it.
And yet there does remain in the logic of European unity a kind of

opposition to, or rivalry with, non-Europeans. In part, it is a rivalry with other primarily white countries like the United States and the Soviet Union. Indeed, arguments about Europe becoming a third "force" or the equal of the two "giants" do go to show that these white rivals are *the* rivals in the short term. But there are also signs of European fears about the long-term effects of Afro-Asian self-assertion, in spite of divisions as between, say, India and China or between the Monrovia and Casablanca groups of African states. The more obvious European fears concern the growth of an Afro-Asian majority in the United Nations—and Lord Home's complaint about "a crisis of confidence" was certainly one expression of them. These fears may well be reflected in the double question: Is Europe yet doing anything to prepare itself for this long-term Afro-Asian challenge? If it is, which of Europe's present actions can be regarded as part of such preparation?

No European leader nowadays is likely to consider it wise to discuss openly the full implications, for Europe's future, of a racially self-conscious Afro-Asia. And yet as influential a columnist as James Reston, writing in *The New York Times,* has claimed that those implications are certainly not absent from European thinking at the highest level. Claiming official sources for his statements he has said that for Britain the need to keep talking to the Russians—and, implicitly, to have a united Europe—arises in part from considerations of future protection against the pressure of races far more numerous than the white races. Looking at the same long-range future, a French official, talking to Mr. Reston, forecast that "the great conflict at the end of the century will not be ideological but racial." [5]

Mr. Reston himself concedes that this may be a wrong forecast but, in his own words, "it is being said, not by broom philosophers, but by some of the most influential officials in the Western world." Mr. Gaitskell, also addressing himself to Americans in reference to Europe and the underdeveloped world, has expressed the fear lest the European Common Market should develop into something "inspired by its own form of nationalism behind a high tariff wall." [6]

But even if Mr. Reston is merely theorizing, Mr. Gaitskell unduly fearful, and the issue of race undiscussed in the counsels of Europe, that issue is still, in the estimation of many Africans, implicit in the logic of European plans. Inevitably, Europeans have both a regional and a racial identity. In American eyes, Europeans may be little more than inhabitants of another continent—cousins, perhaps, across the Atlantic. But to Africans and Asians they are both inhabitants of another continent and members of another race or group of races. European plans that are detrimental to African interests, actually or potentially, cannot therefore avoid racial implications.

*   *   *

At this stage, African objections to the very idea of a united Europe begin to merge into the objection of African association with it—for the detrimental effect on African interests may conceivably arise not so much out of the existence of the European Community as such, as out of the consequences of some forms of African association with it. The United Nations Commission for Africa has expressed a fear shared by many Africans, notwithstanding EEC assurances to the contrary—the fear that "if the associated territories were to try to diversify their economies, by increasing the protection of their local industry against the competition of the EEC, it is doubtful if the EEC countries would continue to offer the same advantages to the export of primary products by the associated countries." [7] The terms granted by the EEC do give those countries freedom to protect their industries by tariffs. What is yet to be unequivocally declared is whether this cheque of "tariffs for protection" is indeed all *blank*—whether the African countries can indeed fill-in *any* amount of protection they themselves consider essential.

There is, in addition, the related danger which the United Nations Commission also noted—that in the transient comfort of associate membership, "the associated African countries might prefer the short-run advantages of tariff concession from the EEC to the long-term advantages of industrial expansion." [8] If this were to happen, nationalists in Africa might well view associate membership of the EEC as just a glorified, twentieth-century version of the African as a "hewer of wood and a drawer of water." Such, at least, was the reasoning of Ghana's High Commissioner to the United Kingdom when he addressed fellow Africans in London in the Spring of 1962. [9] And it is a suspicion that has been repeatedly expressed.

A Western critic, in other ways by no means unsympathetic to African fears, might, however, retort: "If wood is wanted and people are prepared to pay for it, I fail to see what is lost by being a hewer of it." [10] Production of primary products is itself a basis for development, or can be one. The Western capital that, in the nineteenth century, went in search of raw materials in the colonies was an instrument for development in those colonies; and there was thus created what in today's fashionable jargon might be called an "interdependence" between a metropolitan center of industry and a colonial periphery of producers of raw materials.

There have, however, been subsequent and significant changes that have not always been considered in this context. For example, an article on EEC associate membership in 1961 drew attention to the fact that while prices of manufactured goods have been moving slowly upward for a decade or more, the trend of primary products in the same period has too often been downward. Yet the same article found it possible to argue that it was not European groupings which threatened the African economies but rather this instability of commodity prices.[11] If a European grouping were instrumental, if inadvertently, in delaying the emergence of African manufacturing industry and prolonged African dependence on unstable world markets for commodities, it would be difficult not to see the European grouping as at least an indirect threat to Africa's ultimate economic interests. The observation of the United Nations Economic Commission for Africa that unless certain precautions are taken "association with EEC can easily tend to perpetuate economic dependency and thus turn out to be a long-term disadvantage to the country concerned," [12] is at least plausible.

A significant change has in fact taken place from the old "interdependence" between a Europe in the grip of an industrial revolution on the one hand and its sources of raw materials in the colonies on the other. In the initial stages of that interdependence Europe needed her colonies more than the colonies consciously needed Europe. But in the last twenty to thirty years Europe's internal production has grown more rapidly than its need for imports, and some of the previously imported raw materials can now be produced within its own frontiers. Barbara Ward, in her recent study of the economics of underdevelopment in relation to the richer countries, draws attention to the emergence of such items as artificial rubber, new fabrics for textiles, petro-chemicals, and "conceivably even ersatz chocolate." She notes that the Western world's "pull of development" on the outside world has declined in magnitude since the early days of the West's industrial expansion. "We have been filling the gap with extraordinary economic assistance," she says. "But we do not look on this 'job' as a settled commitment. It is still a precarious expedient; and in any case it is too small." [13]

If Western aid is indeed a precarious expedient, arising substantially out of a conceivably transient ideological division within the white world itself, the African can have no certainty about how much longer it will be forthcoming. If Western technology has already produced a number of substitutes for raw materials, the African has no means of knowing how many other Afro-Asian primary products will become dispensable in the wake of a stronger Europe. And even if tropical products remained products exclusively of the Tropics, and Europe continued to have to buy cocoa from, say, Ghana, there would remain an imbalance in this "interdependence" between the producer of cocoa in Ghana and the buyer in Europe. Europe could presumably live without buying chocolate, but could Ghana live without selling cocoa? Could she do so if her economy depended overwhelmingly on cocoa?

Of course, the production of cocoa could be made increasingly efficient. But if this meant greater and greater mechanisation of agriculture, there would presumably come a time when the choice would have to be made between diverting some labor to other industries or producing surpluses on an ever-increasing scale—without adding greatly to the wealth of the country. And Africa as a whole might learn too late that she could not, in President Nkrumah's words, improve even her standard of living by remaining an agricultural continent indefinitely or "improve the skill and ingenuity of her peoples by keeping them solely as workers in rural areas." [14]

Within the context of this reasoning, the EEC freshly underlines the fact that "class" or national income divisions on a global scale coincide with race divisions as between white and colored peoples. To the extent that the EEC has already tempted the bulk of French-speaking Africa with the carrot of associate membership, and may tempt others, the Community can be regarded as one of those devices which President Sekou Touré once condemned as calculated "to make of all Africa the continent of the proletarian peoples." [15]

And if the word "calculated" suggests malicious intent and is unjust to the motives of Europe, then one can, as an alternative, support the view of the *New Statesman* on the EEC and blame at least *"blind* economic forces" for "dividing the world into a white bourgeoisie and a colored proletariat." [16]

      o   o   o

For Africans the problem which thus arises is how to deal rationally with these "economic forces" and avoid a status of excessive economic dependence which, to nationalists, amounts to "neocolonial" status. At the 1962 Cairo Conference of the Casablanca group of African states Sekou Touré felt strongly that both the Monrovia and the Casablanca groups were at least united in their common plight of poverty and underdevelopment, and he was particularly concerned about the need for a common economic policy, both for the sake of economic well-being and as a guarantee of genuine political freedom.

This line of reasoning is not all that far removed from the kind of reasoning involved, at least in part, in the plans of the Europeans themselves. In his article on "De Gaulle's Wider Aims in Europe," in *The Times* [of London] of September 1962, Dr. David Thomson referred to the desire of at least the French to "assert independence abroad." Dr. Thomson confessed that the exact emphasis of the French President's European policy remained in doubt, but the questions which he posed on what that policy might be are themselves significant. "Is (de Gaulle's policy) to create a separate European third force independent of both the super-powers? Or is it, more modestly, to redress the balance within the Atlantic alliance in the direction of less subservience to the United States?" [17]

In either case the move toward European unity seems inspired by the desire to regain for Europe some of the independence that was lost when the balance of power fundamentally shifted following World War II. The Secretary-General of the Italian branch of the Movement of European Federation and Delegate-General of the Congress of the European People, Altiero Spinelli, analyzed the European predicament in precisely these terms in July 1962. He pointed out how economic reconstruction following the war required a central authority for Europe which would distribute aid in a way to promote a balanced recovery of the various countries; how the political reconstruction of Germany had to take place in such a way as not to generate mistrust and disagreement between victors and vanquished; and how military defense and related foreign policies had to be harmonized. But, argues Spinelli, "Europe, founded on the principle of national sovereignties, was organically incapable of undertaking such tasks alone. The American hegemony, willingly accepted by the European States in the dramatic period after the war, supplied the supranational power which Western Europe needed but did not possess." [18]

What this meant was that Europeans were having to give up a little of their old sovereignty—but to someone outside Europe. Certainly, in the area of foreign and military policy, each European government was having to exercise its responsibilities substantially through the Atlantic Alliance—an alliance described by Spinelli as "not a classical alliance but rather a true military confederation." [19]

Of course the United States, too, has commitments to this alliance. But, unlike its European allies, America has had so dominant a place within the alliance that it has been able to preserve "a substantial measure of its sovereignty." [20] It was Europe which faced the agony of choice: the choice "between two forms of supranational power—one constituted by American hegemony, the other by an over-all European government." [21]

It is this choice, seen by Spinelli as facing Europe, that bears a resemblance to the choice which Nkrumah sees as facing Africa, if for the notion of an American hegemony in Europe is substituted the notion of a European or white hegemony in Africa. There is, of course, the further difference that whereas Europe's dependence on America is, at its most *obvious,* dictated by military considerations, Africa's dependence on Europe is more clearly economic. But the essential resemblance in choices is still there—to the extent that a de Gaulle can at least be suspected of looking forward to dispensing with the American presence in Europe and, at the same time, to making indispensable a European presence in Black Africa.

In this latter task he has had a substantial measure of success in some of the French-speaking countries. And this is surely the answer to those critics who keep on asking of Balewa or Nkrumah: "But what could be wrong with associate membership if the French-speaking Africans have willingly accepted it?" Such critics overlook, for one thing, the different colonial backgrounds involved. Long before de Gaulle French colonial policy was based substantially on the idea of the economic integration of the colonies with France. Many of the French territories thus emerged into independence in 1960 finding themselves economically dependent on France to a considerable degree. On the other hand, British colonial policy once stood for, to use Lord Lugard's description, "a policy of equal opportunity (in the colonies) to the commerce of other countries and an unrestricted market to the native producer." [22] This was quite seriously qualified in parts of Africa by Imperial Preference—much to Lugard's disapproval. But even Imperial Preference as a system was more conducive to the economic independence of the colonies than the French integrationist policy ever was. One can almost say that if the term "neo-colonial" had no other meaning, it would have some in the situation in which the French-speaking Africans found themselves on emerging from outright colonialism. Associate membership of the EEC was obtained for them by France while they were still colonies, and was an extension of their original economic integration with the power that had ruled them.

The French-speaking Africans sometimes make a virtue of this necessity. Certainly acceptance of their dependent economic status was facilitated psychologically by that side of French assimilationist policy which encouraged French subjects to identify themselves culturally with France—an identification which today amounts to another "neo-colonial" factor and one which English-speaking Africans may find hard to understand. Indeed, within the reasoning of the English-speaking nationalists, it is all very well for people like His Highness the Aga Khan to impress the Royal Commonwealth Society with a vision that British entry into the EEC may lead, at least in Africa, to an amalgamation of the British Commonwealth and the French Community.[23] To the Nkrumah school of African thinking, the African in the Commonwealth has greater sovereign dignity than the African in the French Community. And an amalgamation of the two may pull down the Commonwealth African to the level of dependence of the French-speaking African rather than pull up, say, the Ivory Coast to the level of self-assertion open to Ghana.

Ghana already does a lot of trade with members of the EEC. But

dependence on France, Germany, Italy, and even Britain as separate
customers was different from a new dependence on them as a unified
economic entity, collectively bargaining for the same terms. Associate membership would formalize this latter type of dependence. The
situation would be worse if associate membership implied, as
French-speaking Africans themselves have demanded, an obligation
not to associate with other groupings which, in effect, Europe might
deem detrimental to Europe. Associate membership might actually
encourage considerable dependence on the EEC[24]—even if it did
fall short of the full integrationist policy pursued by France in
colonial days. Such dependence by itself is difficult to accept in the
estimation of some of the English-speakers. It is even more difficult
to accept if de Gaulle and Dr. Adenauer view the whole European
movement as, in part, a new means of strengthening of the Western
Alliance in its rivalry with the Soviet Union. Being tied to an organization with Cold War competition as *one* of its sources of inspira-
tion may be enough to compromise the policy of non-alignment
which, in spite of the Indo-Chinese conflict, continues to command
allegiance in Africa. It is made worse when, as reported in *The*
[London] *Times* on November 24, 1962, West Germany wants to use
EEC benefits to deter African associates from recognizing East
Germany.

❂   ❂   ❂

We have drifted back and forth between the African objection to
having anything to do with the EEC and the attitude which specifically rejects formal association with it, which is perhaps the most
realistic stand of them all. It is difficult to discuss these latter two
attitudes of objection independently of one another; but there is a
distinction between them worth noting. In part that distinction is
between the use of the term "associated with the EEC" in a formal
sense of membership and the use of the same term in a looser sense
of being allowed to benefit from the prosperity of a united Europe.
It must have been the distinction in this latter sense which impelled
French-speaking Africans to insist at one stage that Commonwealth
Africans should not be allowed to benefit from preferences and aid
provided under the Rome Treaty unless, in the words of an Ivory
Coast diplomat, "they become members of the club." [25] It may be

understandable that these particular Africans should have been concerned about preserving their own privileges. But the question which arises is whether Europe should accommodate them in this matter and declare that poor countries which refuse formal association, or do not qualify for it, deserve no consideration. Are there not, in Dr. Tom Soper's words, "dangers inherent in the richer countries of the world pursuing a program of aid for a selected group of low income regions?" [26] Should not Part IV of the Treaty of Rome be universally applied if Europe is not to penalize some low income countries because of political susceptibilities which Europe itself, through its colonial policies, had helped to bring about?

Indeed, the irony of the matter here is that Europe is offering associate membership specifically to Europe's former subjects, the very people who may be forgiven for being suspicious of any new altruism that smacks of the "White Man's Burden." If European intentions are to help Nigeria, why is it at all relevant that Britain should be a member of the EEC before the EEC would grant tariff concession to Nigeria's hard wood? Surely the implication of this is that an African country can only derive such benefits from the EEC if that country has the credentials of being a colony or ex-colony of a member. The passport to African entry into the EEC must, in other words, bear the mark "Certified as Ex-Colonial Territory of a Member."

It is all very well for Mr. Macmillan to tell British television viewers that he has obtained "excellent terms" for former British subjects in Africa. What was wrong was that the Rome Treaty left it to Mr. Macmillan to negotiate the terms. In other words, the situation was not a straightforward case of Nigeria or Tanganyika qualifying for help because they needed help. It was certainly not a case of a sovereign Tanganyika negotiating directly with the EEC. Rather, it was a case in which it was essential that the ex-colonial Power should speak for Tanganyika—essential even that Tanganyika's former rulers should join the European Club before Tanganyika could get near the club at all as an associate member. Indeed, this need of ex-colonial credentials for associate membership implies that, pending Britain's entry, "only the exports of the ex-Italian part of Somalia can be accepted duty free in Europe and that investments from the [EEC Special Development] Fund can be made only in the ex-

Italian part of Somalia. . . ."[27] And even after Britain's entry Liberia, Ethiopia, and the Portuguese territories would still pose a question mark for the future. For the present, however, the important point is that the apparent need of ex-colonial credentials for associate membership is hardly calculated to allay African fears of "neo-colonialism."

How do these three attitudes in Africa's objections to the EEC together relate to the issue of British entry into Europe? So far as the first attitude of "distrust of the very existence of the EEC" is concerned the African might feel a certain sense of disillusionment, paradoxical and even ironic in some ways, that Britain should want to join such a club at all. And if British entry led to the disintegration of the Commonwealth, the African might feel that, after a brief exercise in sovereign multi-racialism, Britain had turned her back on it. As for the second attitude, that "Europe may do what it wants but we want no part of it," the African may be relatively indifferent as to whether Britain goes in or not, apart from the problem of the loss of the Commonwealth Preference. But as regards the more rational African attitude of "We need to be allowed to benefit by the prosperity of Europe, but not by formal membership of your Club," there is certainly a case for African approval of Britain's entry if this were eventually to lead to the abolition of the very institution of associate membership.

If this were indeed to be the result of Britain's entry into Europe the consequence would be to strengthen those sections of opinion in the EEC which may already stand for devising a more straightforward European contribution to the development of Africa. If this were to lead to a new, unproclaimed concept of the "White Man's Burden," the African nationalist might yet tacitly accept the situation —on the assumption that this new White Man's Burden would be stripped of the racial arrogance and cultural self-righteousness of its predecessor.

NOTES

1. See p. 6 of the Policy Paper.
2. Action Group Policy Paper on the Scientific and Cultural Development of Nigeria, 1960, pp. 1–2.
3. West African Union, *op. cit.*, p. 1.
4. See *The Times* [of London], September 18, 1962.

5. "The Problem of Race in World Politics," *The New York Times,* December 15, 1961.
6. Speech at luncheon of the New York Liberal Party, February 18, 1962. See "Danger of EEC 'Nationalism,'" *Guardian,* February 19, 1962.
7. "The Impact of Western European Integration on African Trade and Development," U.N. Economic and Social Council Document E/CN.14/72, December 7, 1960.
8. *Ibid.*
9. See *Ghana Today,* February 28, 1962.
10. Tom Soper, "Africa and the Common Market," *The Listener,* August 10, 1961.
11. *National Grindlays Review,* 1961. Cited in *Africa Digest,* Vol. IX, No. 6, June 1962, pp. 206-207.
12. E/CN.14/72, *op. cit.*
13. Barbara Ward, *The Rich Nations and the Poor Nations* (New York: W. W. Norton; London: Hamish Hamilton, 1962), pp. 31-34.
14. See *Ghana Today,* February 28, 1962.
15. "Africa's Destiny," *Africa Speaks* (eds. James Duffy and Robert A. Manners) (Princeton: D. Van Nostrand, 1960), p. 37.
16. "The International Class System," *New Statesman,* September 21, 1962.
17. *The Times* [of London], September 12, 1962.
18. "Atlantic Pact and European Unity," *Foreign Affairs,* Vol. 40, No. 4, July 1962, 543-554.
19. "As with other confederations which have meant something in history, this one is viable only because it contains one member 'more equal than others' —indeed, a super-power." *Foreign Affairs,* July 1962, pp. 542-543.
20. *Ibid.,* p. 544.
21. *Ibid.,* p. 545.
22. *The Dual Mandate in British Tropical Africa* (London: William Blackwood, 1922), p. 60. Lugard often quoted Joseph Chamberlain's old idea that the role of Imperial Britain in the Tropics was to act as "trustees of civilization for the commerce of the world," a policy which was supposed to mean "Free Trade" in the colonies with no special advantages for the actual British "trustee."
23. Address given in Cambridge. See H.H. the Aga Khan, "The Great Gamble —In Africa," *Commonwealth Journal,* Vol. V, No. 4, July-August 1962, 187.
24. Parliamentarians from French-speaking Africa, at a conference with the EEC European Parliament in June 1961, argued that the new association envisaged for 1962 (details at the time of writing are still being worked out) should be open to all African states "on condition that none of them should belong to another economic group whose objectives were incompatible with those of the association itself." This version is from *Africa Digest,* Vol. IX, No. 6, June 1962, 205.
25. Quoted by Nora Beloff in "Why the Six Fell Out with the Africans," *Observer,* July 7, 1962.
26. T. Soper, *Commonwealth and Common Market: The Economic Implications,* Fabian Commonwealth Bureau, Research Series 230, September 1962, pp. 14-15.
27. T. Soper, *Commonwealth and Common Market: The Economic Implications,* Fabian Commonwealth Bureau, Research Series 230, September 1962, p. 13.

THE U.S. TRADE POSITION AND
THE COMMON MARKET

Irving B. Kravis

Irving Kravis is Professor of Economics and Chairman of the Department of Economics, University of Pennsylvania. Professor Kravis begins his analysis by examining the many attributes of the United States economy that have provided our exports with competitive strength in the past. Among the most important has been our technological superiority. Recent changes, however, have undermined many of the advantages that American products formerly possessed. He suggests that the impact of the Common Market will further deteriorate our competitive position and might seriously undermine our technological lead. The Common Market has created a substantial amount of economic and political power and the important question to be answered is how will this power be used. He suggests that future American policy will have to take this European power into account.

It is widely appreciated that the terms upon which the United States has participated in world trade during the past century have been favored by unique features of U.S. geography and economic structure. There is reason to fear that some of these past sources of strength may be eroding, owing partly to the continuing revolution in transportation and communication and partly to economic changes both in the United States and in other important industrial countries.

In particular, the economic structure of Western Europe has been moving closer to that of the United States. The United States thus is being made less unique; it is being confronted with keener competition and with a more nearly equal concentration of economic and political power.

This article was prepared for the Joint Economic Committee, Congress of the United States and first appeared as a Joint Committee Print as part of "Factors Affecting the United States Balance of Payments" 87th Congress, 2nd Session. The author is grateful for the helpful comments of Dr. Richard A. Easterlin of the University of Pennsylvania, Dr. Hal B. Lary of the National Bureau of Economic Research, and Dr. Philip J. Bourque, none of whom necessarily subscribes to the analyses or conclusions of the paper.

The European Economic Community (EEC) or the Common Market has accelerated these developments—some more clearly than others. It may not be amiss, therefore, to try to assess the impact of the Common Market upon the United States against this general background of changing relative positions. This approach shifts attention somewhat from the usual emphasis on the dangers of trade diversion that are created by the rapid elimination of trade barriers within the Common Market and the establishment of a common tariff wall around it. Aside from the fact that trade diversion has already been so widely discussed, there are several reasons for favoring this line of attack.

In the first place, the extent of trade diversion itself will depend largely upon the policy choices made by the EEC and these will in turn be influenced by the whole constellation of political and economic power relationships between the EEC and other countries, particularly the United States. This is the more likely since the common external tariff itself cannot be regarded as unduly protective by American standards. Tariff comparisons are notoriously difficult, but it is probably significant that at the rates prevailing in 1960 the average U.S. duty was higher than the common external tariff for 47 out of 74 chapters of the Brussels classification for which data were calculated by the Committee for Economic Development.* Taken in conjunction with the trade-creating effects of the fillip to economic growth given by the Common Market, adverse overall effects on U.S. exports to the Common Market countries will not necessarily follow *automatically* from the existence of the Common Market. Adverse effects may, however, result from the future commercial and economic policies of the Common Market.

Secondly, a discussion of the effects of the Common Market which is concentrated upon trade diversion stresses competition for EEC markets and may omit the important question of competition between EEC and U.S. firms for American and third markets. After

---

* The duties for the various items in each chapter were weighted by the 1960 imports of each area (i.e., the United States and the EEC). Cf., Committee for Economic Development, "A New Trade Policy for the United States," April 1962, pp. 35-38. There is some tendency for the U.S. duties to be higher than those of the EEC on certain raw materials and to be lower on certain finished goods, particularly machinery. This may reflect the greater European dependence on imported materials.

all, U.S. exports to the six account for only about 15 per cent of U.S. commodity exports, and they are, of course, small relative to total sales in the domestic market. Furthermore the more basic issues of relative competitiveness are important also in the contest for EEC markets.

ADVANTAGES OF THE UNITED STATES
IN WORLD TRADE

The historical advantages of the United States in world trade may be listed as follows:

1. By the happy accident of geography the United States had an abundant supply of the materials which constituted the essential requisites of an industrial civilization. Coal and iron were linked by cheap water transport. There were ample supplies of wood. Copper, lead, and zinc were found in quantities adequate not only to supply the United States but also to export to other countries. Abundant supplies meant that materials were cheap and gave a corresponding advantage to manufactured goods.

2. Not only was there a supply of abundant metals but there was also a vast expanse of land variegated with respect to climate and soil. Elsewhere in the world where favorable climate and soil are found, the man-land ratio is generally much higher, and therefore less agricultural output is available for export. Almost from the beginning of the Nation until this day, the United States has thus been a major exporter of agricultural products. It is true that the proportion of our exports made up by agricultural products has been much smaller in recent decades than in the eighteenth and nineteenth centuries but it nevertheless remains a fact that agricultural exports account for one-fourth of the total nonmilitary exports of the United States.

3. The United States **has** been a capital-rich country. The availability of cheap or free land made labor expensive from the beginning, and placed a premium on mechanization. Rough comparisons suggest that in the early or middle 1950's the amount of physical capital per worker used by U.S. enterprises was well over twice as great as that used by the leading countries of Western Europe, while the amount of equipment used per worker was almost twice

as great.[1] While the connection between factor intensities and comparative advantage may not be as simple as was once thought, the abundance of capital in the United States has undoubtedly been an important source of advantage for the United States in world competition. At the minimum a plentiful supply of capital made it easier for American firms to take advantage of the opportunities for large-scale production and made resources more readily available for research and development.

4. The American economy has had the advantage of bold and imaginative entrepreneurs. The combination of a rich and unexploited continent and a high degree of equality of economic opportunity stimulated a vigorous competitive race. While the visible hand of the entrepreneur engaged in self-aggrandizement not infrequently seemed to operate with greater strength than the invisible hand supposedly promoting the public interest, the ruthless entrepreneurs of the nineteenth century did serve to bring about the rapid economic development of the country. They left a heritage of vigor in the adaptation to changing conditions that still permeates American business leadership.

These are the basic factors, but there are two more elements, arising in part at least from some combination of the above, that ought to be mentioned separately.

5. The presence of a domestic market that was both large in size and rich in its capacity to absorb new and high quality products strengthened the export position of the United States. The large American market, combined with the availability of capital and the pressures of competition, stimulated American firms to exploit the advantages of mass production at an earlier date and more extensively than foreign firms. It was the low costs of large size plants that gave the United States the opportunity to enter world markets for many manufactured goods. This was true for standard items such as apparel and farm implements which were produced in other countries by handicraft or small scale manufacturing industries. In addition, however, the wealth of the American market made it possible to cater to a demand for costly and high quality products by developing mechanized methods for their production. This applied not only to consumers' durables but also to the improved machines and materials that were required for their pro-

duction. Countries whose markets would not support the large-scale output of these products imported them from the United States.[2] In a later stage they imported the improved machines and materials.

6. The movement toward the efficiency of mass production may be regarded as part of a broader search for cheaper methods of production and better or new products. In the nineteenth century, the "build a better mousetrap" motivation stimulated a flow of new inventions that were quickly inserted into the economic process. As research and development problems became more complicated, teams of specialists working with expensive equipment began to be developed in virtually every large firm. The result was that the American economy had a significant margin of technological superiority, and in many lines of production U.S. exports depended not so much upon the ability to quote favorable prices as upon the ability to offer qualities, designs, or basic products that could not be obtained elsewhere.

Changes in the American Position

Basic forces operating both in the United States and the world at large seem to be weakening at least a number of these sources of strength in the American position. Let us take them one by one.

1. The advantage of cheap natural materials has been reduced by a number of factors. First of all the voracious appetite of the American industrial machine has chewed up significant portions of the original deposits of many ores. The once rich Mesabi range no longer yields huge quantities of rich ore but mainly the lower grade taconite. Iron ore, like copper, lead, and zinc which the United States once exported to other countries, must now be imported. The new sources of supply—Labrador, South America, Africa, and Asia—are often exploited by international companies in which entrepreneurs from different countries participate, and American buyers have no favored position vis-à-vis buyers from England, Germany, or other countries. Secondly, oil, and natural gas have replaced coal as the lowest cost fuel and the availability of cheap Middle East oil has given our chief industrial rivals an important

if sometimes embarrassing (for the coal-producing countries among them) opportunity to offset the advantage of cheap energy enjoyed by American manufacturers. Third, the advance of technology has reduced the relative advantage derived from having a domestic supply of raw materials. Part of this has been accomplished by the continuing revolution in transport which has been reducing the time and cost required to move heavy materials. Another part stems from the increasing economy in the use of natural materials in industry; according to one estimate, for example, natural inputs declined from 25 per cent of the gross value of manufacturing output in the world's industrial areas in 1938 to 17.6 per cent in 1955. An example of this tendency that has adversely affected the competitive position of an American industry is the reduction in the amount of coke required in the operation of blast furnaces; since coke is more expensive in Europe, the change is more favorable for Europe than for the United States.[3]

On the other hand, the American economy has been a leader in the development of synthetic materials including such important products as artificial fibers, synthetic rubber, and plastics. To the extent that the latest variants of these products continue to be available first and most cheaply in the United States and offsetting advantage with respect to materials is enjoyed by the United States. The possession and extent of such an advantage turns upon technological leadership, discussed below.

2. The potential advantages of the United States in world agricultural markets are frustrated by governmental supports and controls. Although the U.S. Government is scarcely an exception to the almost universal tendency of governments to subsidize and protect agriculture, U.S. agriculture would probably be able to enlarge its export surplus in a free world market. In the world as it actually is, the trend toward increased output behind tariff and quota barriers threatens to limit further the ability of American agriculture to export its products.

3. The U.S. advantages derived from the possession of large amounts of capital have also tended to diminish. One reason— which is of recent origin and may prove to be temporary—is that many of the main competitors of the United States (Germany,

France, and Japan, but not the United Kingdom) have increased their stocks of capital at a faster rate than the United States.* The impact of the differential in growth rates is not, however, nearly so immediate as a different factor which operates so as to minimize the effect of the abundance of capital in the United States. The shrinkage of distance by phone and plane has increased the mobility of capital. The riskiness of investment in Western Europe has been greatly reduced by political stability, rapidly growing markets, strong currencies, and increased familiarity with European laws and business practices. The $18 billion outflow of private long-term capital from the United States during the past decade (exclusive of reinvested earnings) is the equivalent of 2 per cent of the value of reproducible wealth of the United States and perhaps one-fifth that of a country such as Germany, France, or England. (Of course only about one-fourth has gone to Western Europe and a much smaller fraction to any one country, and the comparison with the wealth of these countries is intended only to give an impression of the magnitude of the outflow.)

4. Not only capital but also entrepreneurship has become more mobile; modern technology has expanded the geographical span of control to encompass the world. Thus two-thirds of the long term private capital outflow of the past decade has been in the form of direct investment. Direct investment is accompanied by American entrepreneurship, production know-how, and product design.

5. The increase in incomes in Western Europe and elsewhere has greatly expanded the size of the market and thus the opportunities for mass production of standard products such as apparel, of more costly items such as automobiles, and finally of the improved materials and machines required to produce the higher quality goods. This can be clearly seen in the automobile industry. One of the

* The average annual rate of growth in fixed capital formation in real terms during the decade of the 1950's was 2.1 per cent in the United States compared to 4.5, 4.9, and 9.8 per cent in the United Kingdom, France, and Germany, respectively. The comparison was even more disadvantageous to the United States in the second half of the decade when the U.S. rate was less than 1 per cent. The Japanese rate, available only for the second half of the decade, was 22 per cent. Cf. U.N. "Yearbook of National Account Statistics, 1960," New York, 1961, pp. 265-269.

keys to the new-found ability of the Europeans to meet U.S. competition is a market now large enough to obtain an economical scale of output. In other parts of the world, such as Latin America, where the same techniques of production are available and wage rates are even lower than in Europe, automobile production costs are still high; the market in these places simply is not large enough to obtain the volume necessary for economical output. The dependence of the European automobile industry upon American materials and machines is also being reduced. Originally, a leading German automobile producer bought sheet steel from the United States because the desired quality was scarce in Europe. Now supplies are improving in Europe and prices are lower, and the German company's business may be kept only by special price concessions on the part of the American mill or as a result of a desire on the part of the auto manufacturer to maintain diverse sources of supply.

6. A number of factors have operated in the postwar period to minimize the effect upon international trade of the technological superiority enjoyed by U.S. industry. Shortly after the war, the U.S. Government, for good reasons, encouraged the export of American techniques to other countries. Thus the latest machinery and methods of production were incorporated in foreign plants often built with U.S. funds. In addition, the policies of foreign governments operated to offset the technological advantages enjoyed by the United States. In the first place, certain American companies which were permitted to sell in European markets found themselves holding large sums of inconvertible currencies. Although they had been accustomed to supplying their international operations from American sources, they thus found it desirable to cultivate European sources of supply. In some cases, this involved teaching European suppliers to meet the quality requirements and design specifications that formerly had been available only from American sources. Secondly, many American firms found that they could overcome the barriers of tariffs, exchange controls, and Government purchasing policies only by establishing branches, subsidiaries, or licensees in Europe and elsewhere. More recently, of course, such moves into Europe have been motivated by more purely economic factors, such as higher profit margins, tax advantages, low labor costs, and closer proximity to the market, although tariffs and other

Government policies still play a role. In any case, these establish-
ments have the advantage of American know-how. According to
a British estimate made about a half-dozen years ago, 25 to 30
per cent of company-financed research in the United States was
directly available to Britain through branches of American firms,[4]
and the resources this represented were greater than those spent
by British industry as a whole upon research.

The effect of foreign affiliates upon U.S. exports and the U.S.
balance of payments is not clear. There is some indication of a negative correlation between the expansion of U.S.-owned manufacturing production abroad and U.S. exports for given industries.[5] Even
if this is more firmly established, it is still possible that foreign
affiliates stimulate U.S. exports through purchases of capital equipment, materials, complementary products (to fill out lines) and com-
ponents more than they hurt them. In addition, it is claimed that
foreign producers rather than U.S. home companies would win the
foreign markets if the U.S. producers did not establish the foreign
affiliates. This argument may have long-run validity, but it is weakened at the moment by the fact that the economies of the continental European countries have been working at capacity; it is not
apparent therefore that the European producers would have been
able to expand to take the business now enjoyed by the American
affiliates. Finally, it is pointed out that the foreign affiliates help the
balance of payments by giving rise to a stream of dividends, profits,
and royalties, but this contention is set aside by some who stress
the short-run effects of the immediate investment outlays upon the
balance of payments.

Whether inevitable or induced by governmental policies or by
the profit seeking responses of individual companies, it seems more
probable that the effect of overseas affiliates and licensing will be
adverse for the U.S. trade balance. They certainly appear likely
to accelerate the speed with which knowledge of advanced U.S.
methods is spread throughout the rest of the world.

Of course, these factors work both ways. European affiliates have
been established in the United States and there are American companies that have been licensed to produce European and other
foreign designs that are superior to those available in the United
States. Nevertheless, an increase in the speed with which new

products or methods are transferred is more advantageous for less advanced countries than for those that are in the forefront of technological development.

However, the diffusion of knowledge is scarcely likely to become instantaneous, and it would be of interest to know whether the United States is maintaining its past superiority in developing new methods and products. Research and development expenditures of the United States, it is known, are still many times that of other industrial countries,[6] but it is not known whether the difference is narrowing or not. The importance of this question arises from the fact that the monopoly that an innovating country enjoys on a new product is almost always temporary; even without foreign affiliates or licencees, as knowledge of the new product spreads it is sooner or later successfully imitated abroad. In many cases it will turn out that the innovating country does not enjoy a long-run comparative advantage in producing the new product; thus it sees today's exports become tomorrow's imports. This has happened to a long list of American products from sewing machines to transistors. Furthermore, it is possible that the speed with which innovations are imitated or replaced by superior innovations may be increasing.

If the technological gap between the United States and other industrial countries is, indeed, narrowing, an important source of a demand for dollars is being weakened and the maintenance of our trade position being made more precarious. It is extremely difficult to assess what is happening in this area. One can point to important innovations that have recently come from other countries, but the importation of improved methods is not new. Thus, if one cites the recent import of the oxygen processes for steelmaking from Austria, Germany, or Sweden, it is possible to point to the earlier imports of the bessemer and open hearth processes from England and somewhat later, the extrusion process of squeezing cold steel into desired shapes from Italy. In one area, however, U.S. basic research and development work should be far ahead of that of other countries if the returns are at all proportionate to the investments that have been made—viz, atomic science. If this work begins to produce an economic return the margin of U.S. technological leadership may be strengthened.

More generally, rapid growth in output appears to favor innovation,[7] and a maintenance of the recently developed superiority in the rates of growth of the six and of Japan would not augur well for the United States. Full use of capacity in the United States with the consequent stimulus to investment (foreign as well as domestic financed) and innovation would, on this account at least, be beneficial to the trade balance.

Political Factors

No account of the American position in international trade, however short, would be complete without reference to the way in which it has been fortified by political factors. The relatively small importance of international trade to the American economy and the dispersion of retaliatory power among a fairly large number of trading partners left the United States free to use its great political power to limit or withdraw access to the domestic market whenever foreign producers made inroads that were damaging to American interests. Although the broader political compulsions to which the United States was subjected, especially after the beginning of the cold war, caused this power to be used rather sparingly,[8] the very threat of its use reduced the incentives of foreign producers to make the investment required in many lines of industry to cultivate the U.S. market.

In the last few years, however, the situation has been changing. First, the balance-of-payments difficulties of the United States have for the first time in generations placed it in a position where a sensitive economic nerve was exposed to the good will of other countries. Second, the rise in relative economic power of other countries cannot be ignored. For example, the real gross national product of the five major members of the Common Market expanded from something like 40 per cent of that of the United States in 1950 to 55 per cent in 1960, and if the United Kingdom is added the change is from 60 per cent in 1950 to 75 per cent in 1960.[9] The coalescence of other countries into trading blocs, of which the Common Market is the prime example, has enhanced the significance of these changes. Indeed the formation of these blocs may have a more lasting significance than the difference be-

tween EEC and U.S. rates of growth since the probability of survival is higher for the Common Market than for the growth gap.

THE IMPACT OF THE COMMON MARKET

The forces working against the U.S. trade position thus arise fundamentally from changes in the technology of transportation and
communications and from basic changes in the economic structure
of Western Europe. Western Europe has been the chief beneficiary
of the enhanced geographical mobility of the elements that historically have been primarily sources of American advantage in international trade. Furthermore, Western Europe proceeds toward
Americanization from an internal dynamic as well as from external
effects flowing from the United States. As incomes rise, costly and
high quality products begin to find domestic markets. Domestic
industries arise to cater to these demands, and supplying industries
develop to produce the improved materials and the new machines
necessary to make the new goods.

These changes were flowing at full tide before the advent of the
Common Market at the beginning of 1958, and the new organization has probably added to them only marginally. It is easy to
exaggerate the purely economic impact of the Common Market
upon its members. The Six were growing rapidly before they joined
together as well as afterwards; indeed in the 4 years preceding the
Common Market (1953-57) industrial production in the six countries
combined expanded by 40 per cent and their trade with one another by 78 per cent, while in the 4 ensuing years (1957-61) the
corresponding percentages were 30 and 64, respectively. The real
threat posed by the organization of the Common Market for the
trade position of the United States is the greater concentration of
economic and political power than had previously existed, particularly since there are built-in factors that may cause this power
to be used in ways that will be harmful to American exports.

Before turning to these political aspects, however, let us examine
briefly the respects in which the advent of the Common Market
brings or accelerates economic changes that weaken the U.S.
trade position.

In the first place, the Common Market institutions may have

had some effect in producing more rational practices with respect to certain raw materials than might otherwise have been followed. The complete elimination of tariffs and other restrictions on intra-community trade in coal and steel, achieved under the European Coal and Steel Community (ECSC), reduced transport costs by rationalizing channels of distribution. In coal, for example, mines near national boundaries began to serve areas determined by economic rather than political factors. There are some signs also that the European Communities (i.e., the ECSC, EEC, and Euratom) aided by pressure from the Italians (who have no coal and depend upon cheap oil from external sources), will hasten the process of relaxing restrictions against the import of oil so as to obtain cheap energy supplies despite unfavorable effects on coal. Belgium has surely gone farther in closing down high cost coal mines than she would have been able to do without the political and economic support of the ECSC. Of course, there are some offsetting policies which tend to raise material costs, but these affect mainly tropical products from French-associated areas in Africa and are probably less important in their over-all impact upon materials costs than the policies relating to coal and steel.

Secondly, the Common Market has dramatized the European market and made it more attractive to American capital and enterprise. The Common Market thus has tended to accelerate the process by which American enterprise, technology, and capital rather than American goods move across the ocean.

Third, the formation of the Common Market seems to have provided a stimulus to the growth of large size firms. A wave of mergers, affiliations, and understandings has probably led to larger size and lower cost plants, and has increased the degree of product specialization in plants of a given size. It has led also to larger firms which are more strongly placed with respect to research, finance, and foreign marketing than the smaller ones they replaced. The extent and significance of merger movement in the Common Market are difficult to assess. It is conceivable that what is going on is merely an adjustment by business to the new situation created by the prospect of free trade within the Community. If so, the policy of live and let live, which seems to have characterized Western European business psychology to a greater degree than that of the United States, may soon reassert itself. It is possible that this attitude was as responsible as the inherent limitations of a market of the size of say England or France or Germany for the existence of smaller scale plants than in America. Of course, the EEC has taken steps to implement the anti-cartel provisions of the Rome Treaty, but whether European business will become imbued with a new competitive spirit either through self- or official-inspiration is far from clear. In any case, at the moment there has been a clear gain in efficiency from the rationalization movement that has taken place.

Fourth, the formation of the Common Market has made a contribution to the rate of growth, and thus created a greater market and a greater opportunity for the mass production of standard items and for the large scale production of more costly goods that were almost an American monopoly. In TV and radio, for example, the European market is already on a par with that of the United States in the quality of the product which it can absorb; in most other consumer durables, however, it is 10 to 30 years behind the United States. Of course, the expansion of the European market has been a boon to American exports thus far; it has offset any tendency for trade diversion to hurt U.S. exports. Indeed, U.S. exports to the Common Market have expanded more rapidly than U.S. exports as a whole since 1957 or 1958. However, the European boom can hardly last forever, and when the domestic absorption of European output slackens, U.S. producers may feel the full impact of the new capacities of European firms to produce goods in varieties, qualities, and quantities which formerly could be obtained only in the United States. Many American businessmen fear just this. They feel that their European competitors have been satisfied to follow the price leadership of American firms in the American and sometimes in other markets; this enables European firms, in view of their lower costs, to enjoy high profit margins on their foreign business at a time when their plants are occupied with domestic orders anyway. Of course, if the European countries succeed in maintaining full employment economies with only mild and infrequent recessions[10] further European inroads on markets held by the United States will depend upon the longer-run growth of European capacity.

Finally, the agricultural policy of the Common Market threatens to increase the degree of self-sufficiency of the area by stimulating the expansion of internal production. New export surpluses such as French wheat have already appeared, and if high internal prices are added to the system of variable levies giving preference to Community products, the United States which has been exporting over $1 billion of agricultural products to the Common Market may find itself reduced to the position of a residual supplier especially for grains. Unlike the other factors we have listed, this one involves competition between United States and European producers only for the markets of the Community itself. To the extent that it will affect competition for other markets, it will be unfavorable to the EEC because it will tend to raise the level of costs.

With the possible exception of the last factor, the adverse influences upon U.S. trade that we have discussed thus far have stemmed from economic changes. The most important consequences of the Common Market for the U.S. trade position are, however, likely to flow from a new political fact: For the first time in many decades the United States is faced in the Western World with an almost equal aggregation of economic and political power. The uncoordinated, sometimes conflicting, and often offsetting policies pursued by six governments are being replaced by coordinated decisions reached in Brussels. Even without the addition of new members, the decisions are taken on behalf of countries whose combined importance in world trade already equals or exceeds that of the United States and who provide a significant fraction of the U.S. export surplus.[11] The bargaining power of the Common Market, already substantial, will of course be further increased if Great Britain and other new members and associates are admitted. As the geographical scope of the Common Market is expanded, it will embrace an increasingly diversified area and will become more self-sufficient and less dependent upon external trade than the individual member countries have been. Thus, like the United States, the new entity will have considerable leeway for deciding upon more or less liberal policies.

How will this power be used? Some parts of the answer seem clear. In the first place, the power of the Common Market is likely to be used to retaliate promptly and fully in response to any adverse actions taken in trade matters by another country, including the United States. This has recently been illustrated by the action of the Council of Ministers of the EEC in raising the common external tariff on a half dozen product groups in reprisal for U.S. increases under the GATT escape clause in the duties on carpets and glass. This type of response may be expected not only because of the natural tendency for partners to support an aggrieved member (Belgium, in the carpet and glass case) against an outsider, but also because of the psychology underlying commercial policy in Western Europe. In the latter connection, it is not much of an exaggeration to describe the postwar history of the dismantlement of trade barriers in Western Europe as a story of careful horse-trading in which no concession was given without extracting one of equal value.* In the past, however, retaliatory action by European countries against American protective measures has been infrequent and never so prompt and forthright; countries almost always awaited the negotiation of compensatory concession from the United States to replace the ones that had been withdrawn. The past patience of European countries may, of course, be attributable to the fact that their quantitative restrictions against American goods were still in effect, and as long as this was the case they could not feel quite so ill treated by U.S. actions. However, it may also have been due in part to the absence of a mechanism such as the Common Market which has the power to retaliate effectively and without the fear of the consequences that a small country acting alone would have.

A second factor affecting the use of the power that the EEC has is the inherent tendency of any large area composed of diverse interests to reconcile conflicts over the resolution of domestic difficulties by shifting as much of the burden of adjustment to outsiders as possible. This is evident in U.S. commercial policy. For example, the extensive protection accorded by the United States to its textile industry, including high tariffs and new legislation authorizing the establishment of import quotas, reflects pressures arising from the failure of domestic consumption of textile products to expand as

---

* Perhaps this helps to explain the poor record—relative to that of the United States—of most of the Western European countries in opening their markets to the "low-wage" countries.

rapidly as productivity, with the result that employment levels have been declining. In the short history of the Common Market, there are already a number of illustrations of this tendency to resolve difficulties by cutting off the outsider. These include instances of troubles caused by shortages as well as those caused by surpluses. The most important case involving a surplus, which related to coal, developed in the late 1950's. The desirability of a reduction in imports from the United States and other third countries was virtually the only point on which the Six could agree in their prolonged and difficult negotiations on means of meeting the coal crisis.[12] Analogous action was taken in a number of cases involving shortages; for example, last spring the European Commission recommended to the Dutch Government that it permit the normal volume of potato exports to member countries and restrict exports to third countries.

Even if it seems reasonable to suppose that the Common Market will retaliate when the occasion arises and shift the burden of adjustments to third countries when internal difficulties develop, there remains a large and important area of doubt about the way in which the Community will wield the great power which its size and importance confers upon it. Although the Rome Treaty contains a clause stating that the member countries intend to follow a liberal commercial policy (art. 110), the commitment is quite general and could conceivably be subordinated to other objectives of the Six. At the risk of some oversimplification, one might say that there are two schools of thought within the Community on this matter. One school, for which the French are the spokesmen on many issues, takes the view that the Community represents, among other things, a club for the mutual benefit of the member countries at the expense of outsiders. This position has been generally opposed by the Dutch and also by the Germans, both of whom tend to prefer more liberal trading policies for the Community. Of course, the difference is one of degree, albeit an important one, because some element of tariff discrimination in favor of fellow members is the essence of a customs union. While it is true that the conception of the EEC goes far beyond a mere customs union, it is also true that the most immediate practical attraction of the EEC to participants and would-be participants is its customs union feature.

There is, however, ample room for differences in emphasis, and this may be seen in the positions taken on a number of important problems by the French on the one hand and the Dutch and Germans on the other hand. For example, the French generally resisted the efforts of the Benelux countries and Germany to obtain exceptions from the common external tariffs* in the form of tariff quotas for products formerly obtained from third countries. The French argued that Community sources of supply should be sought and developed to the maximum extent possible, while the Dutch and the Germans wished to maintain their former trade ties. In the outcome, about half of the 150 requests for tariff quotas were granted; the common external tariff was reduced in some of the other cases. (The 150 requests covered about 2¼ per cent of EEC imports from third countries in 1960.[13])

Another issue in which the difference in viewpoint played an important role concerned the margins of preference to be accorded the products of associated countries and territories, particularly tropical products from African areas. The issue arose recently because the initial 5-year arrangement with the associated territories and countries had to be renegotiated. The French wished to maintain high common external tariffs, thus affording the associated African areas a sheltered position in the markets of the Community. The Dutch and the Germans, whose imports from Commonwealth and other non-Community African areas were three or four times as great as their imports from associated areas, favored low common external tariffs. The compromise that appears to be emerging involves moderate or low external duties offset by enlarged subsidies for the associated areas.

Conclusions

There are a number of basic developments that seem to be reducing the strength of the American position in international trade. The exhaustion of some low-cost domestic sources of material sup-

---

* Actually, the exceptions were sought from the duties that would have to be established in the course of the first movement toward the common external tariff, as the treaty provides that the members are to adjust their duties to the common ones in a series of three steps.

plies and economies in the use of natural raw materials have reduced the margin of advantage enjoyed by the United States from the availability of cheap natural raw materials. The American comparative advantage in agriculture has been offset by governmental policies that limit increasingly the ability of the United States to market its agricultural products commercially. The greater geographical mobility of entrepreneurs and of capital and the more rapid dissemination of new techniques and new products have dispersed to many countries, especially those in Western Europe, important elements of strength that formerly favored the United States. The growth of income and wealth in foreign countries, particularly in Europe, have made it more possible for foreign producers to take advantage of the economies of mass production, and sizable foreign markets have begun to develop for high cost quality products which formerly could be marketed on a large enough scale to warrant domestic production only in the United States.

The advent of the Common Market has strengthened many of these adverse economic tendencies, but, more important, it has created a center of political and economic power that can retaliate against any increase in American protection and that may in any case be driven to use its power to exclude foreign competition. There are in the Common Market, just as in the United States, divided opinions on the choice between protectionism and liberalism. A distinct choice of one position or the other by either entity would undoubtedly have strong repercussions on the other's policy.

It is possible, of course, that these losses of advantage may be offset by a new flowering of innovations, particularly in various fields of application of atomic science, such as energy, medicine, and telecommunications.

Even if this does not occur or if its impact is too small to offset fully the other adverse effects, it does not mean that the United States would be left without a comparative advantage in a significant range of products. Indeed, the rapid growth in trade between the more nearly equal partners of the Common Market suggests that trade need not rest upon large differences in economic structure.

However, as far as the Atlantic Community is concerned, such trade would be trade between equals rather than trade between a technological leader and a number of other countries none of which has so high a per capita income or so extensive a market. The real terms of trade that can be maintained by a technological leader are superior to those that can be attained by one of a group of equals. The reason is that the leader's currency is placed at a premium as a result of its power to command goods that cannot be obtained elsewhere.*

Even a sharp adverse movement in the terms of trade would hardly have severe effects upon the real income of a country such as the United States whose imports are equivalent to less than 3 per cent and exports to less than 4 per cent of its gross national project. The real problem would be to find the optimum means for the necessary adjustment in the terms of trade to take place.

If the United States has to accept less favorable terms of trade, there are two ways in which this can be accomplished. One way is to depreciate the exchange value of the dollar in terms of other currencies. This possibility has been receiving increasing attention recently both in terms of a one-time devaluation and in terms of establishing a free or floating rate of exchange. Either of these alternatives would tend to weaken the strength of the forces that are moving the world toward a higher degree of economic integration.

The other way is to increase the internal purchasing power of the dollar relative to that of other currencies while keeping exchange rates fixed. This used to be discussed entirely in terms of an absolute deflation of prices and wages, and in such terms it clearly is not politically feasible. In a world of rising prices, however, the same result can be achieved by confining the movement of the price level to a smaller rise than that which takes place in other countries. It may not be too much to hope that one focus of the international monetary cooperation which is developing in the Western World will take the form of coordination as well as consultation concerning the relationship between price movements and balance-of-payments necessities; countries in surplus might be en-

---

* There are many different concepts of the terms of trade. The simplest, which will serve for our purposes, is the one which measures changes in the terms of trade by dividing an index of export prices by an index of import prices. The commodity terms of trade, as this concept is called, tells us what are the changes in the quantity of imports we obtain for one physical unit of exports.

couraged to loosen wage and price reins, and those in deficit to tighten them. Relative price movements in the right direction, from the standpoint of the U.S. deficit, have occurred in the last few years, whether influenced or not by international cooperation.

On the political side, the main implication that has to be drawn from the rise in the political and economic power of Western Europe and particularly the Common Market is that the United States is no longer able with impunity to adjust its tariff and trade measures unilaterally to meet difficulties arising for domestic industries.[14] While the postwar trade record of the United States is no worse and in some respects better* than that of most other industrial countries, there is a larger gap—which has been well publicized—between the trade philosophy consistently preached by all our postwar administrations and the invocation of quantitative restrictions on such things as dairy products, lead and zinc, and oil and the increases in tariffs on such products as watches, bicycles, and glass. The result is that the United States is not in a strong moral or political position to oppose the inherent tendency of the Common Market to act in a similarly protective manner when confronted with its own internal problems. Furthermore, more than two can play, and there are other—though less powerful—countries and blocs ready to enter the game.

If it turns out in fact that other countries or groups become more ready to withdraw concessions and to retaliate when the United States withdraws them, the United States will have three alternative courses of action. One is to accept the fact that other nations like the United States will resolve conflicts between domestic interests and international obligations rather consistently in favor of the former. This course, however, would lead to the fragmentation of the Western World and to a trade jungle, and it may be rejected out of hand.

A second possibility is the acceptance by the United States, and other countries, of tighter controls over escape clauses. This would involve a sharp departure from present GATT practice, under which the unilateral invocation of escape clauses tends to be highly permissive. Tighter controls can be achieved either by developing spe-

---

* See the previous note on the treatment of goods from low-wage countries.

cific and detailed criteria which must be satisfied before the escape clause can be invoked, or by establishing some international control over the act of invocation. The former has been tried only in Benelux among the major international arrangements affecting trade matters, and then only temporarily; it is too difficult to develop in advance objective criteria that will be satisfactory for every situation. Experience in Benelux, the OEEC Code of Liberalization, the European Coal and Steel Community, and the European Economic Community thus favors international authority over invocation rather than an attempt to devise objective criteria which will effectively narrow the scope for unilateral action.

International control over the invocation of escape clauses may take many different forms. The group of member countries in a new or revised GATT might, for example, have the right to veto unilateral invocation by say a two-thirds vote. An illustration of an arrangement that would vest more stringent control of the use of escape clause in the group of nations would be to provide that the escape clause could not be invoked without its prior concurrence by a majority or by a two-thirds vote.

In view of the widespread opposition and fear that such a proposal would undoubtedly raise, it is worth stressing that the experience in organizations referred to above invariably indicates a reluctance on the part of the member states to use the power of the group, even when the existence of such power was explicit, to impose a course of action upon any national state whether the issue related to an escape clause problem or anything else. Of course, the existence of the power of the group, even though it not be used, alters the psychological and political framework within which a safeguard program is resolved. It makes it less likely that domestic pressures will prevail as easily as when safeguards may be invoked unilaterally.

A tomorrow will have to come when the Western World will move in this direction, but there is a third alternative that may seem preferable at the moment, especially to those who vehemently oppose any measure that smacks of the surrender of U.S. sovereignty. This is to devise trade expansion commitments in broad terms, leaving each country with considerable freedom both to select the items upon which concessions will be made and subsequently to make substitutions. The commitment might consist of the obligation to achieve a given percentage reduction in the average rate of duty collected on imports as a whole or one each of a number of categories of imports. Some duties could be subjected to less-than-average and others to more-than-average reductions, so long as the over-all target percentage cut was attained. Furthermore, when a particular duty reduction turned out to create unanticipated difficulties it could be withdrawn and another substituted for it as long as the required average reduction was maintained. Placed in a framework of the steady movement of average duties toward lower levels, the selection of the most innocuous duty reductions as those made first will matter little. Similarly, freedom to make substitutions, unless grossly abused, will facilitate the transition to freer trade without creating areas of permanent protection.

*   *   *

In summary, an important aspect of the balance-of-payments problem facing the United States is the growing equality of other foci of political and economic power. The establishment of the Common Market has contributed significantly to the political phases of this development. The economic phases appear to be rooted in the dynamics of the Western European economy, and the Common Market has merely added a further stimulus. These developments will require a period of readjustment in relationships. On the political level they leave the United States with less freedom of action than it had before, and on the economic level with the need to accept poorer terms of trade unless there is a burgeoning of a new technological revolution that is uniquely American.

NOTES

1. These statements are based on rough calculations made from data in R. Goldsmith and C. Saunders (editors), "The Measurement of National Wealth," Income and Wealth, Series VIII, London, 1959, and M. Gilbert and associates, "Comparative National Products and Price Levels," Paris, 1957.

2. S. B. Linder has recently stressed the role of domestic demand in conferring a comparative advantage upon a country for a given product. Cf. his "Essay on Trade and Transformation," New York, 1961, especially pp. 87-91.

3. GATT, "International Trade, 1955," p. 12.
4. J. H. Dunning, "American Investment in British Manufacturing Industry," London, 1958, p. 167.
5. "Survey of Current Business," September 1961, pp. 23-24.
6. For example, a recent comparison of the United States and British research and development expenditures concluded: "After adjusting the exchange rate to get a comparison which is, as near as possible, in real terms, it seems that American industry's research expenditure is over five times as large as British industry's, as an absolute figure; it is nearly three times as large per employee, and twice as large as a percentage of net output." See C. Freeman, "Research and Development: A Comparison Between British and American Industry," Economic Review (National Institute of Economic and Social Research, London), May 1962.
7. Cf., J. Schmookler, "Economic Sources of Inventive Activity," Journal of Economic History, March 1962.
8. See my paper in the Harvard Business Review, March-April 1962.
9. Based on rough extrapolations of U.S. price weighted estimates given in M. Gilbert and associates, "Comparative National Products and Price Levels," Paris, 1957.
10. See the paper by Milton Gilbert and the discussion by Walter Salant in the May 1962 American Economic Review.
11. In 1961, for example, U.S. exports to the Six were $3.5 billion and imports from them were $2.2 billion, while the over-all U.S. trade surplus was $5.3 billion. OECDE, "Foreign Trade," series A, April 1962.
12. This case is more fully discussed in my book entitled "Domestic Interests and International Obligations," University of Pennsylvania Press, forthcoming.
13. Bulletin of the European Economic Community, September-October 1961, pp. 39-45.
14. Materials in the remaining paragraphs are drawn largely from the author's "Domestic Interests and International Obligations," in press.

UNITED STATES AGRICULTURAL EXPORTS
AND THE EUROPEAN COMMON MARKET

Charles S. Murphy

Charles Murphy is the Under Secretary of Agriculture of the United States. This statement was presented by Mr. Murphy on December 12, 1962 in testimony before the Subcommittee on International Exchange and Payments of the Joint Economic Committee, Congress of the United States in the hearings on the outlook for the United States balance of payments. Mr. Murphy began his testimony by recalling the great strides made by American agriculture and suggested that these technological gains have won for the United States an important export market. He indicated that the rapidly rising level of income in the Common Market presents the United States with an opportunity for expanding U.S. agricultural exports to them. Mr. Murphy pointed out, however, that the agricultural policies being adopted by the Common Market may well prevent the U.S. from reaching this potential and may take away part of the market the U.S. already has. He suggests that the United States may meet this challenge through direct negotiations with the EEC.

I am pleased to meet with you today to discuss the role of agricultural exports in the U.S. balance-of-payments position and the outlook for such exports, especially as our trade may be affected by the European Common Market.

How all our efforts to cope with the balance-of-payments problems are seriously threatened from a new direction—the European Common Market and its retrogressive steps in agricultural trade. Our exports of agricultural commodities to Western Europe constitute an essential element in the U.S. balance of payments. This agricultural trade is approximately equal to the trade deficit that the United States will have this year in its over-all international balance. This deficit was incurred primarily to meet our security and assistance commitments in Western Europe and other areas, and any sizable cutback in the volume of our agricultural trade would seriously impair our ability to maintain these commitments.

In other words, the role of agricultural exports is considerably broader than that of helping to maintain a sound American agricultural economy.

The United States, as we all know, has a tremendously productive agricultural plant, and from that plant we are exporting about 15 per cent of the production. This compares with about 8 per cent of our nonfarm production sold in foreign markets. For the year ending June 1962, agricultural exports reached a record total of $5.1 billion. This total includes both exports for dollars and exports under Public Law 480. If Public Law 480 sales are deducted, then dollar agricultural exports account for about 20 per cent of our total merchandise export earnings.

During the past 5 years, there has been a marked growth in the value of our farm products sold abroad for dollars as compared with imports of agricultural commodities that are directly competitive with our own production. The aggregate value of our exports of such commodities exceeded our imports of such commodities by $5.4 billion over these 5 years, which amount is shown on the credit side of our balance-of-payments ledger.

We have consistently exported more competitive agricultural products than we have imported. This fact eloquently attests to the efficiency of American farm production. There are some who suggest that this balance is maintained through the use of extensive import controls on these competitive products. Let me correct this erroneous notion.

We have been fairly generous in past trade negotiations in granting access to our markets for competing agricultural products. These concessions have been granted in exchange for concessions we have obtained from other countries on our exports, often industrial exports. The results add up to a liberal trade policy on our part with respect to agricultural imports.

Import controls limiting the quantity which foreign suppliers can sell in the U.S. market are applied today on only five agricultural commodities—cotton, wheat and wheat flour, peanuts, certain manufactured dairy products, and sugar. And the domestic production of all these commodities, except dairy products, is likewise controlled. All other agricultural imports of the United States, which include fresh and frozen beef and lamb, pork, a large variety of canned meat products, vegetable oils, fruits and vegetables, tobacco, and even feed grains, are permitted unrestricted entry and are subject to only moderate tariffs.

Our farm productivity and efficiency have put American agriculture in the export business, and it is there to stay. From early history, we have relied on cotton and tobacco for our major agricultural export earnings. Now these historical exports must share the limelight with other American products. Today, we find these export earnings swelling rapidly through our increased sales of soybeans, feed grains, poultry, and fruit. We look to a further substantial expansion of the commercial exports of these and other products provided we get improved access to markets abroad. Not only is it necessary to obtain the relaxation or removal of nontariff barriers which presently impede our trade, but it is imperative that foreign governments refrain from applying protectionist measures which nullify our competitive advantage and deny U.S. farm products a reasonable opportunity to compete in their markets.

It is sometimes suggested that a more extensive use of export subsidies would substantially increase our agricultural exports and result in a significant contribution to meeting our balance-of-payments difficulties. We have used export subsidies primarily where needed to maintain our fair share of the world trade in certain commodities. We now make export payments on a limited number of products. We feel that if used indiscriminately, export subsidies could not only seriously disrupt orderly international trade, but could also endanger our balance-of-payments condition. Any undue disruption of trade patterns might bring about retaliatory measures not only against the subsidized product, but against our industrial exports as well.

You will note that I refer particularly to an expansion of our dollar trade. There are really two types of markets for our agricultural exports—the markets in the developed industrialized countries where we sell for dollars and the markets in the developing countries where the bulk of our sales are on concessional terms. In the latter countries, we will continue to seek ways to share our abundance to relieve hunger and to encourage economic growth. By using the productivity of our farms to hasten economic development, we build the commercial markets of the future. This has already been demonstrated, for example, in the case of Spain, which used to be a large Public Law 480 customer for our soybean oil. It has now become a dollar buyer of this product. This year, Spain's dollar purchases of U.S. soybean oil will amount to over 400 million pounds, valued at about $45 million. It is now the largest single export outlet for our soybean oil.

Japan presents an even more dramatic example. Only a few years ago, a large part of our agricultural sales to Japan were made under Public Law 480 for local currencies. Now Japan has a booming economy, and last year was our largest dollar export market. It is a market we value very highly—one that has the potential of further substantial expansion, one where the Trade Expansion Act of 1962 will be of material assistance to us in further improving terms of access.

It is our dollar exports—trade with the so-called developed countries, and particularly with the Common Market—that I would now like to discuss. In fiscal year 1962, Canada, Japan, and the United Kingdom were grouped closely together as the leading individual exports markets for our farm products. Each bought about $500 million worth of agricultural products. Also in 1962, as a group the six members of the Common Market bought about $1.2 billion of U.S. agricultural commodities out of total U.S. dollar exports of $3.5 billion. Indicating this is a rapidly growing market, our agricultural sales to the Six in fiscal year 1962 were 35 per cent greater than in fiscal 1958. During the 1958-62 period, our feed grain and soybean shipments to the Common Market have more than doubled. From 10 million pounds in calendar year 1958, our shipments of poultry, mainly to West Germany and the Netherlands, rose to 160 million pounds in calendar year 1961.

The rapid rate of growth and the booming economy of the Common Market, attributable no doubt in large part to their developing economic unity, have afforded us increased potential outlets for our farm production. Prosperity in Western Europe has brought increased demand for meat, poultry, milk, and eggs—a demand that has expanded livestock and poultry numbers. U.S. grain has been imported to supply the additional feed required. We foresee that as the economy of this area becomes more prosperous, there will be an ever-increasing demand for food and fiber. However, there is a grave question as to who will be allowed to supply this increasing demand—and, indeed, as to whether the United States and other third countries will not have the doors of historic trade closed in their faces.

The prospects for a continued outlet for our agricultural exports will be determined in large part by the evolving common agricultural policy of the EEC. We are disturbed by the mounting evidence that this policy will be regressive and trade restrictive. We have been urging that the Common Market develop its common agricultural policy along lines consistent with the maintenance of international trade. By this we mean that it should formulate its agricultural policies so as to maintain a level of international trade consistent with principles of fair competition having due regard to its position as a major importer of agricultural commodities and a major exporter of industrial products. Such a policy is not only required in the interest of fairness to friendly agricultural exporting countries, such as the United States, but in the interest of the Common Market itself.

Industrialization in Western Europe has historically been aided by the importation of moderately priced agricultural and other raw materials from outside the area. Its industries as well as its consumers have greatly benefited from this practice. We want to see it continued. The formation of the Common Market has ushered in a new period of economic growth which can be continued and even accelerated if its consumers and its factories continue to have access to moderately priced agricultural imports.

Our hopes for liberal policies are being realized on some products. These are the products which the Common Market does not produce at all, or produces in small volume. These include cotton, soybeans and soybean meal, tallow, hides and skins, certain fruits and vegetables, and some other farm products. These commodities represent about $700 million worth of our farm products shipments to the area. For these products, the EEC proposes to apply a fixed common external tariff. The prospects are bright that our exports of these products as a group will expand as that trading area expands. However, even for these commodities, trade is not entirely free of problems. For some products, the duties are still high. To safeguard our trade, we will need to negotiate a reduction in the common external tariff of items such as tobacco, vegetable oils, and canned fruits and vegetables.

For the remainder of our current trade with the Common Market, amounting to nearly $500 million, we are concerned over our future prospects. This includes our trade in wheat and wheat flour, feed grains, certain meat products, poultry, eggs, and rice. The reason for this concern is the emphasis placed by the EEC's common agricultural policies on variable levies and minimum import prices rather than on fixed tariffs. This levy system is designed to make possible unlimited protection to domestic production and could readily be used for the deliberate purpose of promoting self-sufficiency.

The first Community-wide regulations for agricultural commodities went into effect on July 30, 1962, for wheat, wheat flour, feed grains, poultry and eggs, certain fruits and vegetables, wine, live hogs, and hog carcasses. Regulations for other livestock products and rice are expected to follow shortly.

The regulations for wheat, flour, feed grains, poultry, eggs, and pork—all items of important trade interest to the United States—establish variable levies to replace the previously existing tariffs and other trade regulating mechanisms. These levies will vary from time to time and to the extent necessary not only to equalize the price of the imported products with the EEC's internal domestic prices but also to afford a price preference for the marketing of domestic production. Domestic prices, most of which are already high, will be fixed by government action. Under this system, a non-member supplier—no matter how efficient he may be—can never get a price advantage over the domestic producer when the variable levy is applied. It is the purpose of this device to equalize the cost of imports with the predetermined level of internal prices. EEC producers will be guaranteed a market for all they can produce at the price levels fixed by the governmental body. The pressures for high internal prices will be great. The use of this system to maintain high internal target prices could provide a powerful stimulus to uneconomic production and a substantial decrease of imports.

It is a complicated mechanism, as necessarily it would have to be, to bring the external levies to a common level eventually. It varies from commodity to commodity. It is implemented by an extremely complex set of regulations. Many of us find that we experience a difficulty in understanding our own regulations. And I am inclined to suspect that the people who administer these variable levies have the same kind of problems with their regulations.

But the purpose of the system is to provide whatever level of protection is necessary to give an advantage to encourage producers. The levy works against any import price. They decide what the target price is internally, and generally speaking they add an amount equal to the difference between the target price and the import or world price to the world price, or a little bit more, to protect the target price. And that is the way the system works.

Wheat, flour, feed grains, and poultry products account for most of the value of the U.S. exports that will be affected by the variable import levy system. In the marketing year 1961-62, our exports to the EEC of wheat and flour were $121 million; feed grains, $271 million; and poultry and eggs, $67 million. Trade data now available do not enable an evaluation of the impact of this system on our trade in wheat and feed grains since its adoption on July 30. Due to the overprotection afforded by this system, our trade in flour has virtually disappeared. There has been a substantial slowing down of our sales of poultry and egg products since July 30. This is due primarily to the application of levies and minimum import prices which has resulted in an import charge of about 12.5 cents a pound on poultry by West Germany, our major market, in place of a duty of about 5 cents a pound charged before July 30.

The combined value of these exports approaches $500 million. The loss of any substantial part of these exports would have a serious effect upon our balance-of-payments position.

A comparison of import charges—where valid comparisons are available—clearly shows the extent of the increase in levels of protection for those commodities about which we are especially concerned. The following table illustrates selected examples of import levies in major markets for certain commodities before and after the common agricultural policy became effective.

In the case of the Netherlands, the levy on wheat prior to July 1 was $3.19 per (metric) ton.

After July 30 it was $33.24.

For wheat flour it went from $14.50 to $49.60.

For corn, from $16.67 to $18.63.

For barley, from $16.67 to $21.03.

Sorghums, $16.67 to $21.07.

In the case of Germany, the levy on wheat went from $42.50 to $61.25.

On corn, from $46.05 to $55.20.

Barley, from $35.69 to $49.40.

Sorghums, $45.84 to $55.15.

And on poultry, from about 4.5 to 5 cents to 12.5 cents a pound.

You can readily see how these radically increased burdens on U.S. imports will play havoc with existing trade patterns.

The amount of our trade threatened by the common agricultural policy would be increased if the United Kingdom should become a member of the EEC. In fiscal 1962, our agricultural exports to the United Kingdom were about $500 million. If the variable levy system of the Common Market were applied to the United Kingdom, it would affect $130 million worth of those exports to the United Kingdom of grains and certain livestock products. For most of our other trade with the United Kingdom, duties are substantially lower than in the Common Market. The extension of the Common Market to include the United Kingdom without any changes in the present features of its common agricultural policy would therefore substantially impair our terms of access to the United Kingdom market.

How can we meet this trade challenge posed by the Common Market? Today, the issue hangs in the balance. The way is open, and we hope the Community will not irrevocably cast the die in favor of retrogressive protectionism.

As we seek to meet this challenge, we find the status of specific commodities to be as follows:

In quality wheat, we have an interim agreement with the Common Market that if the common agricultural policy results in a decline in our historical trade, action will be taken to correct this decline. We are keeping this matter under continuing examination to determine the need for this corrective action.

Flour: We have a small but steady trade in flour with the Netherlands. This is fast disappearing because of the overprotection given flour through the variable import levy system. We have urged moderation of this protection. We have not yet gained our point.

Rice: We have stressed the trade-damaging effects that a proposed variable levy system could have. Our efforts have been supported by the interests of certain member countries and thus far, the variable levy system has not been put into effect.

Tobacco and vegetable oils: The Common Market officials are well aware of our dissatisfaction with the tariff levels negotiated at the last trade conference in 1961. We have their assurance that they will be prepared to consider reductions at our next tariff negotiations.

All wheat, corn, grain sorghum, and poultry: At our last tariff negotiations with the Common Market, we kept the door open for further negotiations on these items. With respect to poultry, strong representations have been made by President Kennedy to Chancellor Adenauer on the potential harmful effects of the sharp rise in the protection given poultry in West Germany. The German Government is now considering action which we expect to lead to a reduction in the levy. We are urging the Common Market officials either to eliminate the minimum import price feature of this system, or to reduce it substantially.

We have had numerous discussions with Common Market officials and pointed out that under their levy system, the key element is that of the level of prices set by the Community. We have urged that they demonstrate their declared intentions of following a liberal trade policy in agriculture by establishing moderate price levels for their grain products. This would retard expansion of uneconomic production and permit trade to continue with efficient producers.

There has been increasing emphasis by the Community officials in these discussions on the need for international commodity arrangements to deal with some of these troublesome agricultural trade problems. On our part, we believe that international commodity arrangements merit consideration, if they are designed to preserve legitimate trade patterns. We are willing at the proper time to seek to negotiate such arrangements. We have indicated our desire that a meeting be called early in 1963 under the auspices of the GATT in an attempt to negotiate a grain agreement. Our objectives as an exporting nation would be to obtain reasonable access to the Common Market. This might be accomplished by any one or a combination of several methods, including maximum limits on variable fees and assured import quotas.

We do not look upon commodity agreements as a substitute for normal rules governing world trade in farm products. Trade in the widest possible range of agricultural commodities and foodstuffs should continue to be regulated by conventional means of moderate fixed tariffs, tariff quotas, and limits on levies. We firmly believe that the international trade rules for agriculture should not be permitted to drift away from the rules which apply to international trade generally. In other words, countries should seek to carry out their trade policies in accordance with the provisions of the GATT, which apply to industry and agriculture alike.

In this connection, at the last GATT meeting, we sought the enforcement of these rules on certain countries who continue to restrict imports of our farm products. The GATT countries recognized our complaint against France and approved the withdrawal of compensatory benefits by the United States if France did not remove its restrictions within a reasonable time. A similar action against Italy was suspended when Italy removed some of its restrictions. This represents the first action by the United States to threaten withdrawal against other GATT partners if illegal restrictions were not removed.

We propose to insist upon fair treatment.

We have built into the fabric of highest U.S. policy a determination to preserve reasonable access to the Common Market for our agricultural products. For many months we have been expressing through diplomatic channels and publicly our apprehensions about the emerging EEC agricultural policies. Secretary Freeman, on November 19 before the Agricultural Ministers of the OECD in Paris, expressed these apprehensions most vigorously.

At that time, Secretary Freeman warned our European friends that they must be internationally minded in developing their agricultural policies. He pointed out that decisions of the EEC will be the most important single factor in determining whether the world continues to move forward toward more liberal international trade policies, not only for agriculture but for industry as well.

We cannot—

the Secretary said—

be internationally minded in industrial areas of our respective economies, but nationalistic and overly protective in the agricultural sector. Either the two great sectors must move forward together under liberal trade agreements, or both will in time succumb to protectionism.

Under Secretary Ball of the Department of State repeated this U.S. policy the following week in Paris at the Foreign Ministers' meeting of OECD.

It is only within such a framework that we will be able to use the Trade Expansion Act of 1962 to promote more liberal trade arrangements. We have a mandate by the Congress to use this act to gain access for our agricultural commodities. This is evident from the section 252 provision.

The Trade Expansion Act gives us bargaining power to offer broad and deep tariff cuts to the Common Market in exchange for concessions on agricultural exports from us. Equipped with this bargaining power, we may be able to obtain access to their agricultural markets, including those protected by the variable import levies, if we make it clear at the outset and throughout our negotiations that fair solutions for these agricultural trade problems are an indispensable part of the tariff and trade package we mean to negotiate.

The wrong agricultural policies in Europe could negate the opportunities to use the provisions of the new trade act. As Secretary Freeman said, we cannot negotiate reductions in our industrial tariffs while at the same time we are denied access to markets for our agricultural exports.

It will be a great pity if Common Market officials fail to recognize that the trading countries of the free world will not permit agricultural trade to retreat behind high tariffs and protective devices. The expanded EEC would be a dominant factor in world trade in agricultural products. Friendly countries should be able to look to it to assume a proper position of responsibility and set a trade example which their trading partners can follow. These countries, as equally concerned as the United States over their agricultural trade with the expanded community, are looking for U.S. leadership in the forthcoming tariff negotiations under the Trade Expansion Act. There is an increasing awareness that if this act turns out to be a meaningless instrument in the field of agricultural trade, and the Common Market persists in providing excessive added protection for its own agricultural programs at the expense of outside supplies, the economic and political unity of the Western World will be seriously affected.

PART IV

The Challenge and the Future

HOLD FAST

Paul-Henri Spaak

Paul-Henri Spaak is the Minister for Foreign Affairs of Belgium. He was formerly Secretary-General of NATO and three times Prime Minister of Belgium. M. Spaak is concerned in this article with the rupture of the negotiations for British entry into the Common Market. He reviews the history of British relations with the European integration movements up to the French veto in January 1963. He then analyzes the possible reasons for the action by General de Gaulle. In reply to the question of what should be done now, M. Spaak suggests that the principles of European unity should not be compromised and that progress will come after the delay caused by current French policy passes.

I

It becomes clearer and clearer that January 14, 1963, is fated to go down in history as the "black Monday" of both European policy and Atlantic policy. What occurred that day was something much more significant than the mere dooming of negotiations between Great Britain and the European Community. It was, in plain fact, an attack on the Atlantic Alliance and the European Community— an attack, that is, on the two most significant achievements of the free world since the end of World War II.

"Hold Fast" by Paul-Henri Spaak from *Foreign Affairs* (July 1963). Copyright by the Council on Foreign Relations Inc., New York. Reprinted by permission of the Council on Foreign Relations.

Those who have been active in international politics since 1945 must sometimes wonder whether they have done better or worse than those who were in power after 1919. It can be said quite objectively, I believe, that they have done better. They adapted themselves—though not without some difficulty—to the formidable process of decolonization; they created NATO, the greatest defensive alliance the world has ever known; and by setting up the Common Market they halted the process of deterioration which was beginning in Europe. If it be added that the likelihood of a European war which might grow into a world war now seems very remote, one might conclude that there was no reason to be too dissatisfied.

But the decision taken by General de Gaulle on January 14 puts all this either directly or indirectly in jeopardy.

We must begin by analyzing the method which he used to break up the negotiations with the British, the pretexts given and why the true reasons were concealed. When we have ascertained what the real reasons were, we shall be ready to draw conclusions regarding such a dangerous diplomatic action.

II

The background of the problem can be sketched rapidly. For a long time—for too long a time—Britain refused to accept the idea of a united Europe. Its hesitations and procrastinations are regrettable, but the reasons are understandable: a great country which has just won a great war is naturally reluctant to acknowledge that it must radically alter its age-old traditions. The mere fact of victory works against the effort of readjustment.

Great Britain accepted the Council of Europe with reluctance. It deliberately refused to take part in the Coal and Steel Community. It stayed out of the discussions on the European Defense Community. It chose not to participate in the negotiations which were to culminate in the Common Market. For a long time it did not believe that the European idea would work, and it would not abandon its traditional views and policies in order to embark on what it deemed to be a hazardous adventure. But the European Coal and Steel Community was formed, the Treaty of Rome was concluded and ratified, and the European Commission was set up. The achievements of the new organization were as swift as they were sensational.

During this time, the British Empire was falling apart and both economic and political relations among the Commonwealth countries were becoming less important. The hour of agonizing reappraisal was drawing near. It struck in 1961.

Mr. Macmillan's Government understood that it had to choose, and it made its choice with courage. In October 1961, Mr. Heath declared in Paris that his country was ready to accept the principles of the Treaty of Rome, with the attendant political consequences. He added that the three main problems involved in Britain's entry into the Common Market were: the existing ties between Britain and the Commonwealth countries; British agriculture; and the interests of the European Free Trade Area. The six members of the European Economic Community, France included, declared that they accepted this statement of the problem and agreed to open negotiations on the basis of it.

Was France ready at that time, or was she not ready, to admit Britain into the Community? No categorical reply can be given. What is certain is that France executed a triple play designed to make it more difficult for Britain to enter the Common Market. France invented a procedure for the discussions which contained dangers that I, for one, perceived at once. Britain should have been regarded as a possible future partner and treated as we had treated each other when discussing the Treaty of Rome. Instead, it was decided that the Six as a group would negotiate with Britain standing by itself. Throughout the negotiations, therefore, there were double parleyings, first among the partners of the EEC, and then between them and Britain. In preparing for the Treaty of Rome we had set up a Committee of the Whole on which all the partners were represented and which sought mutually acceptable solutions; this time we were adversaries confronting each other without having suggested possible solutions.

During the talks among the Six, France cleverly insisted on a strict interpretation of the provisions of the Treaty of Rome. This naturally hindered the granting of exceptions and accommodations which Britain asked for, and such as we had generously accorded to ourselves. France also demanded that real negotiations with Great Britain should not begin until after agricultural policy had been settled within the EEC and until after relations between the EEC and the African countries had been regulated. France knew that by hardening the position of the EEC on these two points it would be erecting obstacles which Britain would find it hard to surmount.

Without giving the matter enough thought, even those who were most in favor of Britain's entry into the Common Market accepted these tactics. In such circumstances the negotiations were bound to take a long time, and did. But long and difficult as they were, progress was made. The relations between the EEC and the Commonwealth countries were practically settled. With only a few exceptions, Britain adopted the EEC's external tariffs. Finally, Britain agreed to align its agricultural policy with that of the EEC by December 31, 1969, at the latest.

Two full weeks of further discussion were planned to begin January 14, 1963. Optimists among the negotiators hoped during this period to reach the final stage which would open the way for the British entry. A few days before the beginning of the session, Mr. Fayat, Belgium's Deputy Minister of Foreign Affairs, went to Paris to settle the details of the proceedings. Everything went smoothly. He returned to Brussels very pleased with the talks he had had. The negotiators met as scheduled on January 14. Nothing gave them the slightest hint of the bombshell that was about to explode.

On the afternoon of January 14, General de Gaulle held a press conference at which, to everyone's stupefaction, he propounded two ideas: (1) Great Britain was not ripe for admission to the Common Market; (2) the Brussels negotiations, having reached a deadlock, should be terminated. The effect in the conference was dismay, confusion and also anger.

There can be no doubt that the method employed was totally inexcusable. I have never heard anyone—anyone at all, not even the most loyal Gaullist—attempt to justify it. Not only was the method inexcusable as regards Britain; it was equally inexcusable vis-à-vis France's five partners. One simply cannot comprehend how negotiations begun by general agreement among a group of six nations could be broken off at the wish of one member of the group without any previous discussion, or why a press conference should be chosen to make this wish known abruptly to its partners.

Let it not be said that this procedural aspect is secondary. I regard it, on the contrary, as very important. It reveals General de Gaulle's open contempt for the views of his partners and at the same time a will to make his own views prevail at the expense not merely of the rules of common civility but of the rules by which a community must be governed. When one partner in an organization like the European Community thinks it natural to impose its will on all the rest, nobody can be surprised if the spirit of collaboration languishes.

Certainly the concept of the European Community which lies behind this "diplomatic method" is a highly individual one. In General de Gaulle's mind, the partners in the Community are not really equal, as the founders had planned. What we are witnessing is an attempt by one partner, who regards himself as the strongest, to impose his own will on the others. In the coming year, however, the partners have no intention of accepting such treatment.

III

It will long be argued whether the negotiations with Britain might have reached a successful outcome or whether they were in any case doomed to failure. No definite answer can ever be given. The only way of discovering whether negotiations will be successful is to pursue them to the end. That is what General de Gaulle would not permit.

Of all those concerned, only the French believed that the negotiations would fail. France's five partners in the Common Market, Great Britain and the European Commission were unanimous in taking the opposite view. Though the negotiators realized that difficulties existed and that there were still important problems to be solved—even tackled for the first time—all who took part, except the French, laid greater emphasis on the ground already successfully covered. All except the French foresaw the possibility of a satisfactory final settlement.

But further controversy on this point is futile, not only because it can never be decided, but chiefly because it soon became apparent that the two grounds cited by the President of the French Republic for terminating the negotiations were only pretexts; the real reasons lay elsewhere.

When we search for these real reasons I do not think that anyone can deny today that the Nassau agreement between Great Britain and the United States was the underlying cause of General de Gaulle's decision. Doubtless he had never been enthusiastically in favor of Great Britain's entry into the Common Market; but judging from his attitude between October 1961 and January 1963, he was reluctant to show his hostility openly or to take direct responsibility for the failure of the Brussels negotiations. He would certainly have preferred them to fail for technical reasons. The Nassau agreement seems to have been a new element in the situation which caused him to explode his bombshell on January 14.

I believe that, as he saw it, the British at Nassau had the choice between a nuclear policy pursued in close collaboration with the United States and a European policy carried out in collaboration with France. By choosing the first, Britain definitively cut itself off from Europe.

From this we may deduce that the key element of General de Gaulle's doctrine, the one which has the highest priority, the one which shapes his international policy, is his determination that France shall have her own nuclear *force de frappe*. All those who do not help him to carry out his "grand design" must therefore be against him. For myself, this is not a new view of General de Gaulle's policy; I already held it when I was Secretary-General of NATO.

General de Gaulle's thinking might be summed up in simplified form as follows: "Every great country must have its own nuclear deterrent. France is a great country. Therefore France must have her own nuclear deterrent." I am convinced that nothing will persuade him to advance beyond the stark simplicity of this syllogism. Because the United States did not accept it, Franco-American relations within NATO deteriorated. Because Britain would not adhere to it at Nassau, the doors of Europe were shut in its face.

I do not share either General de Gaulle's ideas on the French *force de frappe* or his concept of the defense of the free world. Before I explain my reasons, however, let me note two arguments in support of his thesis which I think carry some weight:

1. It is difficult to suppose that great European countries such as Great Britain and France can be completely excluded from the formulation of nuclear strategy and from the execution of it in time of war. Their standing in the world, their history, their great military traditions all speak against their being reduced to such a secondary role. It would be all but impossible to get them to agree that in a war in which their existence was at stake they were to have no say on its most important aspect.

2. To abandon the idea of building up a national *force de frappe* would very probably mean the closing of important avenues of progress in certain scientific and industrial fields which are today of paramount significance. The fact is (and it does not do us honor) that most of the vast sums needed for scientific research and development can be obtained only through military budgets. National defense is often the only reason that seems adequate to justify many kinds of expenditure. Considerations of national defense are what have enabled the United States and the Soviet Union to take the lead in the conquest of space. One must either imitate them or renounce the pursuit of that tremendous adventure.

Both arguments, I repeat, are sound. True, the United States has made an effort to meet the first, at least indirectly. Its proposals for an inter-allied nuclear force or a multilateral nuclear force within the framework of NATO would certainly furnish a basis for collaboration in which the largest allies would participate in making nuclear strategy. And in fact it is inconceivable that there should not be close cooperation between the NATO and the American forces. Nevertheless, the American proposals as they stand have not solved the crucial question as to which authority is entitled to make use of the nuclear weapons. Thus far, the famous question, "Who will push the button?" remains unanswered. It seems to me, however, that an answer can be found.

On the other hand, the problem created by the scientific and industrial knowledge that may be acquired through military research in atomic and electronic fields remains wide open. I have thought for a long time that this is the weakest point of the Atlantic Alliance. When I was Secretary-General of NATO, I used to say: "Is it really essential to European pride that Europe discover again what was long ago discovered in the United States? And on the other hand,

would the security of the United States be jeopardized if it told its
friends secrets which are already known to its enemies?" This great
gap in the field of collaboration, this refusal to share knowledge
which extends beyond the scope of military needs, is the chief reason
for the difficulties we have mentioned, and to some extent it justifies
the French attitude.

In the interests of objectivity, I hasten to add that General
de Gaulle's frequent allusions to the temporary nature of the Atlantic
Alliance and his repeated references to a Europe stretching from the
Atlantic to the Urals are not of the kind to inspire great confidence
on the part of the United States Government. Secrets can be shared
only with an unconditional ally.

IV

General de Gaulle's television speech of April 19 sheds further
light on his concepts. Twice at least, in seeking to justify the crush-
ing financial burden which he asks the French people to assume in
order that he can build up his nuclear *force de frappe,* he stated
that the effort was necessary in order to defend France if it were
attacked. This brings us to the crux of the problem.

The planning of a military organization, and the tactics and
strategy for its use, must be based on a set of political assumptions.

It seems to me that from the political standpoint General de Gaulle
visualizes a future war as a virtually unaltered repetition of what
happened in the wars of 1914 and 1939: France is attacked—and I
presume that in his mind the Communists this time take the place
of the Germans. Such a conception strikes me as entirely outdated.

In my view, if a third world war occurred, it would have nothing
in common with the wars we have known. It would not be fought
for the purpose of restoring frontiers, or of territorial conquest, or
of economic expansion. A third world war could have no other objective than to fulfill the Communist desire for world domination, and
in such a conflict Europe would play only a secondary part. If,
contrary to the ideas expounded and defended by Mr. Khrushchev
—for which we should be grateful to him—Communism should one
day decide to resort to war in order to achieve world supremacy,
the country it would have to attack would be the United States. The

Communists know that the outcome of the conflict could not be decided in Paris, Bonn, or London, but only in Washington; consequently, France would be attacked only to the extent that all of Europe was attacked, and the United States at the same time as Europe.

The Atlantic Alliance was founded on the principle that the defense of the free world, on both sides of the Atlantic, is one and indivisible. This principle remains valid today, and it is my profound conviction that this political reality should determine the form of our military organization. This means, I believe, that the military organization should become steadily more closely integrated.

To these various considerations should be added General de Gaulle's expressed belief that sooner or later the United States will withdraw its armed forces from Europe and that as it becomes increasingly concerned with its own security in a narrow sense it will refuse to employ its nuclear weapons in the defense of its allies. This is contrary to the constantly repeated declaration of the American leaders. Apart from the fact that it may be somewhat dangerous to keep on questioning their words, it seems to me inconceivable that the United States would allow Communist forces to overrun all of Europe when obviously this would be only a first step toward the next goal—that of knocking out the United States itself.

I might add that it is rather difficult to imagine the Soviet Union starting a war with Europe, in which it would risk sustaining serious damage, while leaving the United States out of the conflict with all its forces intact and capable of intervening when and as it chose.

All these various theories and assumptions seem to me mistaken. They fail so plainly to take into account the real situation that exists in the world today, the forces in being and the goals that might be sought, that I wonder whether they do not conceal a line of rather complicated political thinking. I wonder whether in reality General de Gaulle is not seeking to speed the departure of the American forces from Europe, since he regards it as in any case inevitable. The void thus created might lead the other European countries to take refuge under the sheltering wing of France, which then alone could afford them some protection. This would be tantamount to a French hegemony in Europe, the achievement of the Gaullist grand design.

If such is the notion, then it is indeed composed of dreams and idle fancies. It is a completely outdated notion, an anachronism. It looks back to the policies of centuries past and rejects the two major ideas which have dominated international life since the end of World War II: the building of a united Europe and the global defense of the free world.

V

What conclusions are we to draw from all this? Without dramatizing the situation, we must recognize that the Atlantic Alliance and the European Community are going through the most serious crisis they have so far experienced.

One of their largest members, France—or at any rate, official France—no longer believes in the two basic principles which led to the formation of NATO and of the Common Market. It no longer believes that the defense of the free world is indivisible, and it is looking for a substitute formula. It also does not believe in the community spirit which animated the authors of the Treaty of Rome. The French concept of the Europe which must now be created is a sort of alliance, with the bonds between the partners no closer than those which held the Triple Alliance together before 1914. Paris may attach a little more importance now to cultural and economic matters, but if so it is only a little seasoning added to very ancient recipes. We are thousands of miles away from the concept of a federated Europe, where each country would retain its basic national characteristics while pooling what the modern world requires must be handled in common—international policy, defense and economic policy.

There is much more here than a difference in tactics. The differences are of fundamental principle. In such circumstances there is but one thing for NATO and the European Community to do: hold fast. We must be faithful to the rules laid down for NATO in 1948 and for the Common Market in 1957. We must persevere and not give way.

Within NATO, this means basically that in the political field we must consult together more and more closely on a widening range of problems, with a view to evolving a joint Atlantic policy. It means that from the military standpoint, after establishing a set of principles and determining the eventuality for which we must prepare, we must integrate conventional and nuclear means of defense to the highest possible degree. That will be the best reply to those who doubt the indivisibility of defense.

Within the European Community, we must continue the work auspiciously begun. If possible, we must skip some stages of tariff abolition, advance rapidly toward a common policy in trade, transport, and social affairs, tackle the great monetary problem, work out an agricultural policy, and, by avoiding autarchy and protectionism, demonstrate that the European Community is an open organization.

These ideas are still held today by the overwhelming majority of European statesmen. They are shared by the overwhelming majority of European peoples. Let us not, then, be dismayed.

If we review in our minds the policy of the Western world during the years following World War II, we still, in spite of everything, arrive at the cheering conclusion that there is no need to change its main lines. Some details of application must be altered. But it is not an agonizing reappraisal that is called for, only an intelligent evolution based on experience. The dissident element constituted by current French policy may be a cause of delay, but it cannot prevent the ultimate success of the great undertakings to which Europe and the United States have set their hands.